ENTREPRENEUR
Power Plays

ENTREPRENEUR
P o w e r   P l a y s

How the World's Most

Dynamic Thinkers

Reach the Top of Their Game

M c G r a w – H i l l

New York · Chicago · San Francisco
Lisbon · London · Madrid · Mexico City · Milan
New Delhi · San Juan · Seoul · Singapore
Sydney · Toronto

This publication is designed to provide accurate and authoritative information in regard to the subject matter covered. It is sold with the understanding that neither the author nor the publisher is engaged in rendering legal, accounting, or other professional service. If legal advice or other expert assistance is required, the services of a competent professional person should be sought.

—*From a Declaration of Principles jointly adopted by a Committee of the American Bar Association and a Committee of Publishers*

McGraw-Hill books are available at special quantity discounts to use as premiums and sales promotions, or for use in corporate training programs. To contact a representative please visit the Contact Us pages at www.mhprofessional.com.

This book is printed on acid-free paper.

INTRODUCTION

BusinessWeek readers tell us how busy their professional lives have become and how important it is to get their business news, information, and ideas delivered in a concise and authoritative fashion. We do that each week in the magazine, and every day at BusinessWeek.com. But we also know that businesspeople need to delve deeply into areas that will help them manage more effectively. That's why we have created the Power Plays series in collaboration with McGraw-Hill Professional books. Each book draws from *BusinessWeek*'s in-depth reporting on exceptional leaders as they face strategic challenges on a variety of fronts.

The Power Plays chapters address real-life situations where best practices are at work in companies large and small. To make the narratives more useful, we have distilled information designed to help enhance your performance in today's complex business environment. This information is presented in readily digestible nuggets: "Lesson Plans" that articulate the key points of the case study, "Power Moves" that deliver tactical advice on how to manage change, and "Monday Morning" strategies that focus on achieving success and keeping progress rolling.

This Power Plays volume highlights remarkable entrepreneurs who are running their own companies as well as energetic managers forging an entrepreneurial style within larger organizations. It's an impressive lineup: Larry Page and Sergey Brin were tinkering with a new formula for searching the Internet as Stanford University students when they developed the technology that spawned Google. Golf Pro Greg Norman wasn't content with stellar performance on the golf course alone; he created a diverse portfolio of businesses that generate hundreds of millions in revenue each year. Another pro,

Johnathan Wendel, a top player in the virtual world of electronic games, aims to turn a niche phenomenon into a mainstream sport viewed by millions. At startup Digg.com, Kevin Rose is determined to avoid the mistakes of the year 2000 dot-com implosion and prove that a successful Web 2.0 company can be launched with minimal seed money. In a world where Starbucks rules, David Schomer, convinced that there's room for another cultish brew, has launched his chain of Espresso Vivace Roasterias.

Rapid growth has spawned a class of aggressive entrepreneurs in China, as well. In one case study, we survey the Mainland's hottest consumer products and the people behind them. Elsewhere, we meet China's Yuan Yuanqing, who is striving to make electronics giant Lenovo as nimble as a small company, as he melds the best of Chinese and U.S. business cultures.

Not surprisingly, many of the best examples of entrepreneurial zeal are found in Silicon Valley, so we visit there often. Superstar Jeff Bezos shows how constant reinvention is the key to Amazon's success. Versatility turns out to be at the core of Linus Torvalds's unique business model, one that turned Linux from a geeky start-up to a Microsoft rival. At Linden Labs, understanding the obsessions of the virtual community is a big reason for the success of online star Second Life. In Paris, Apollonia Poilâne's tasty products and continuing innovation have brought a new burst of energy to her family-owned bakery. Across the channel, London designer Misa Harada's fashion lines are the rage among the celebrity set.

In the fast-growing service industry, vigilance and an ability to think ahead of emerging problems have propelled Robert Funk's Express Personnel to powerhouse status in the talent management industry. Preaching environmental sustainability has been the key to growth for Sun Rank entrepreneurs Roger and Cynthia Lang.

We round out this volume with some thoughts on how the MySpace Generation lives, buys, and plays online. We hope this provocative piece will rev up your entrepreneurial thoughts and energies.

One note about these case studies: They are drawn from *BusinessWeek* reporting at the time the stories were written, and therefore are snapshots in time. Every effort has been made to provide factual updates, but some of the characters and circumstances upon which the studies are based have changed. Still, we believe that these narratives stand the test of time and remain not only illuminating but replete with valuable lessons for developing successful power plays.

* * *

Many people at *BusinessWeek* contributed the ideas and case studies in this book including Michael Arndt, Frederik Balfour, Peter Burrows, Beth Carney, Bruce Einhorn, Ben Elgin, Dean Foust, Amber Haq, Jessi Hempel, Robert Hof, Stanley Holmes, David Kiley, Sarah Lacy, Paula Lehman, Stacy Perman, Dexter Roberts, Michael Shari, and David Schomer. Frank Comes, Jamie Russell, Jessica Silver-Greenberg, and Craig Sturgis developed the series with Mary Glenn and Ed Chupak, our colleagues at sister company McGraw-Hill Professional. Commentaries were provided by Pamela Kruger. Very special thanks go to Ruth Mannino for her excellent guidance on design and editorial production.

Stephen J. Adler
Editor-in-Chief
BusinessWeek

BusinessWeek

ENTREPRENEUR
Power Plays

SERGEY BRIN AND LARRY PAGE: KEEPING THE EDGE AT GOOGLE

LESSON PLAN

Zealously protect the brand and maintain the organization's high standards so that consumers remain loyal.

Inspire bold, new ideas by injecting fun into the workplace and giving employees the freedom to work on pet projects.

Stay ahead of the pack by not imitating competitors, but instead continuing to emphasize breakthrough innovations.

Keep in mind that consumers want technology to be easy to use, reliable, and fast—not just "cool."

POWER PLAYERS

In the late 1990s, Stanford University computer science students Larry Page and Sergey Brin began tinkering with an explosive idea: scanning the topology of Internet links to determine a page's popularity. Thus began Google, which offered a quantum leap forward in search technology.

Ben Elgin's 2004 cover story (with Jay Green and Steve Hamm) looks at how Google's start-up management style could help it defeat all its competitors.

1

BLAZING A NEW PATH

The spring sun shines brightly on the so-called Googleplex, the five-building campus of the hottest Internet search engine on earth. At lunchtime, hundreds of engineers at Google Inc. chow on free fare prepared by the former chef of the Grateful Dead. Kicking back? It's more like a fuel stop. They eat, paying little heed to cofounder Larry Page as he swoops by on skates. And as evening sets in, those same brainiacs, wedged three to six per office, huddle in quiet conference or patter away at their computers in unblinking concentration. Whether in sneakers or on skates, the Google crowd emits cerebral intensity and an almost palpable sense of urgency.

You'd think they would be celebrating. All around the world, Web-surfing humanity has found its way to Google's bare-bones Web site and picked up the simple formula, pecking out a few words and hitting enter. Google has blazed a new path of learning and turned its search engine into the key to knowledge. Its massive banks of servers process more than 3,000 searches every second of the day. Now, much of Silicon Valley is waiting eagerly for the miracle company to translate its soaring popularity into a mountain of cash. As soon as late April, Google could file papers for an initial public offering, the first marquee tech IPO since the collapse of the dot-com bubble three years ago. Google, which analysts believe topped $900 million in sales and $150 million in net profits last year, could raise $1 to $2 billion. The whole company may be valued at $20 billion by the public market—easily a record among Internet IPOs. "Google has proved a better mousetrap matters," says Microsoft Corp. CEO Steven A. Ballmer.

EMPHASIZING INNOVATION

But Google's payday is arriving just as the search phenomenon faces a withering battery of tests. The company's spectacular success has lured brawny competitors such as Microsoft and Yahoo! Inc. into the arena. Those companies view search as a command center of the Internet, and they plan to wrest it from the upstart in Mountain View, California. The result will be a battle for the heart of the Net—one just as momentous as the browser war between Microsoft and Netscape Communications that took place a decade ago. Says Roger McNamee, managing partner at venture capitalist Silver Lake Partners, which has no stake in Google: "Search is the key to the kingdom."

And the battle is raging at Google's ramparts. Yahoo is leading the assault. In February, the portal giant fired up a new search engine that analysts say nearly matches Google's performance. More worrisome, Yahoo CEO Terry S. Semel is driving Yahoo to the next frontier, customized search. Instead of today's one-size-fits-all searches, he wants to offer queries tailored for an individual's tastes, interests, even location. Advertisers are ready to pay royally to reach this type of targeted audience. And Yahoo is off to a big head start in gathering the personal information necessary to deliver such customization. It has amassed 141 million customer profiles, Google next to none. "They're quite vulnerable," says Michael A. Cusumano, professor of management at Massachusetts Institute of Technology.

Even if Google sidesteps that threat, it faces another, perhaps more daunting one. Microsoft is working to leverage every bit of its Windows monopoly in its effort to win the search market. Ballmer and Chairman William H. Gates III are working to embed search capabilities into nearly every aspect of future versions of the operating system. Have a question? Search the Web and the hard drive too from a Word document, an instant chat box, even an Excel spreadsheet. There's no need to pay a visit to a search site. If Microsoft makes good on this sweeping expansion, it could turn Googling into a quaint ramble down memory lane.

POWER MOVE

Like most successful start-ups, Google faces stiff competition from Microsoft and other well-financed giants. But rather than trying to follow in its rivals' footsteps, Google keeps its edge by emphasizing innovation, creating breakthrough products and technology.

Google's trials would strain even a battle-hardened outfit geared for war. But the company still operates under freewheeling management, a vestige of its peaceful prosperity as a private company. Under a ruling triumvirate, no one executive has clear control. CEO Eric E. Schmidt, 48, was hired three years ago to provide experienced leadership. But his role, as he describes it, sounds more like a chief operating officer's than a CEO's. He says he handles "the day-to-day stuff," making sure the right people are talking and reaching out to partners. Decisions emerge from three-way negotiations between Schmidt and cofounders Page and Sergey Brin. It's the founders who chart Google's path, wielding veto power over strategy and technology moves. Engineers, meanwhile, work in the same culture of controlled chaos that built the start-up. All are free to pursue their own pet projects. The result is an engineer's dream—but hell for planners. Some investors find the approach unsettling. "They do not sound even remotely like a fiercely competitive world-class company, [but] rather kids playing in a sandbox," says one Google investor, who plans on selling shortly after the IPO.

POWER MOVE

The conventional wisdom is that large organizations need to be governed by one person; otherwise, chaos will ensue. But by making big decisions by consensus, Google cofounders Sergey Brin and Larry Page and CEO Eric Schmidt have been able to avoid making big mistakes.

LEADING BY CONSENSUS

The kids will have to grow up fast. Not only are their giant rivals knocking off Google's search engine, but they're also plugging it into just about everything they offer, from e-mail to job boards. This is an attempt to outflank Google and turn search into a ubiquitous feature, a commodity. To defend its market, Google must come up with a better model, one that establishes its search engine as a central platform for computing. This pushes Google to extend from its slender specialized base and venture into many of the same broad services that the giants offer. To keep the big powers from feasting on its specialty, Google must stretch and become a sprawling power of its own.

This is leading Google executives to weigh ideas that to some may seem dire in nature. For example, Jeffrey D. Ullman, a computer science professor at Stanford University and a member of Google's four-person technology advisory council, says he's urged the company to acquire or team up with a Linux desktop company so that Google can extend search to information stored on the computer. This means competing head-on with Microsoft's dominant Windows operating system. "If Google doesn't reach the desktop," cautions Ullman, "Microsoft will eventually take Google's business, just like it took Netscape's." Google executives say that they've discussed the possibility but aren't poised to act.

POWER MOVE

Leaders need to understand the risks involved with innovation. Google was blindsided when its new, free e-mail service—which offered far more storage than competing services— was fiercely criticized for including advertisements.

With such intense competitive pressure, Google's management could be stretched to the breaking point. Considering how rarely co-CEOs have been able to share an executive suite effectively, experts think it's only a matter of time before the power-sharing setup at Google dissolves. "If multiple people are making decisions, decisions don't get made," says David Yoffie, a professor at Harvard Business School. "At Google, there are tens or hundreds of projects going on simultaneously. Ultimately one person has to make a decision."

Schmidt responds that Google's consensus-management structure, while maddening at times, is effective. It combines Page and Brin's technology expertise and his own operations experience. "We try to run as a group, because partnerships make better decisions," says Schmidt, adding, "It's very, very lonely if you're the only person with a very hard decision to make." He takes exception to the idea that he acts like a COO. Rather, he compares Google to Yahoo and auction titan eBay, where the founders shaped the strategic vision, although they didn't have the title of chief executive officer. "I've tried very hard to have this be a founder-driven company," he says. "It's what most other high-tech companies have done."

Schmidt's supporters say that the CEO's style may send an inaccurate signal about his power in the company. "Eric likes to be self-deprecating," says Bill Campbell, chairman of Intuit, who has served as a management adviser to Google for $2^{1}/_{2}$ years. "He's not the COO. He's the CEO of the company and does a good job of it."

Google executives also maintain that the company's freewheeling engineering culture is not a liability but an asset. To offset Microsoft and Yahoo's crushing advantage in size, scope, and customers, they say, the far smaller Google requires breakthrough innovations. The company, which receives about 1,000 résumés a day, has hired hundreds of engineers and scores of top-ranked Ph.D.s in recent years. By giving these people free rein to pursue new ideas, Google expects to come up with services, from e-mail to community networks, that will set its larger competitors back on their heels. "What we really talk about is how we can attract and develop this creative culture," says Schmidt. "Innovation comes from invention, which you cannot schedule."

The Google team dished up a fresh serving of its trademark audacity on March 31 when it announced a new e-mail service known as Gmail. The service will offer users free e-mail with one gigabyte of storage—250 times as much as its nearest competitor. But it comes with a catch: a bold and controversial proposal to introduce advertising into e-mail. Google's computers will sift through correspondence and place related advertisements in the margins of e-mails. Gripe about your busted toilet in an e-mail, and the note is likely to come with an ad for plumbing supplies. It's classic Google: imaginative, provocative, and capable of obliterating the status quo.

DAMAGE CONTROL

But with the launch of Gmail, the young company unwittingly put its own naïveté on display. Instead of basking in the glow of the new service, Google's harried press relations team had to shift quickly into damage control as 28 privacy and consumer groups blasted the company. They complained that plans to scan the text of letters constituted an infringement of privacy. Cofounder Brin was pressed into service, calling up media outlets to make Google's case. This kind of scrutiny is new to the company, which has long been a darling among consumers.

POWER MOVE

At great companies, ideas don't just emanate from the top; they also percolate up from the bottom and middle levels. At Google, engineers are encouraged to spend one day a week working on pet projects. No idea is deemed too off the wall to pursue.

The Gmail hiccup has done little to dampen the Googlemania sweeping Silicon Valley. The upcoming IPO promises to deliver the kind of bonanza the Valley has been aching for since the dot-com bust. According to researcher Venture Economics and sources familiar with Google's financing, venture firms Kleiner Perkins Caufield & Byers and Sequoia Capital stand to turn their $10 million investments of five years ago into about $2 billion each. Cofounders Brin and Page could be worth more than $3 billion each. Even executives at rival Yahoo are licking their chops. The company invested $10 million in Google four years ago for a stake that could be valued at roughly $300 million. Investors, meanwhile, are lining up to buy Google shares. "I love this company. I love this business," says Duane Roberts, head of equity strategy at Dana Investment Advisors, an asset manager in Brookfield, Wisconsin. "This is going to be another one of the blue chips, like eBay, Yahoo, and Amazon."

It's likely to be valued as one. Back-of-the-napkin analyses circulating in Silicon Valley put a $20 billion valuation on Google. Assume that it notched $150 million in net profits last year, as analysts estimate. Most of that comes from search marketing—

an industry that is projected to grow by 70 percent in 2004. If Google maintains its share, which analysts say is likely, net profits could pass $250 million in 2004. That would give it a price-earnings ratio of 80, only a tad below Yahoo's P/E of 87. Some analysts are skeptical. "I wouldn't want to see Google come out at the same valuation as Yahoo," says Allison Thacker, a portfolio manager at RS Investments, a San Francisco–based money manager. "Yahoo has a powerful franchise that provides an array of services to consumers. Google doesn't really have that at this point."

POWER MOVE

One way to promote creativity is to make the workplace fun. Google offers perks like $4,000 Segway scooters to get around the campus and $800 digital toilets that have remote controls to adjust the seat temperature.

FOCUS ON CREATIVITY

Google executives are betting that their technological expertise will help them make up the difference. Page, 31, is the son of a computer science professor and a database consultant, while the Russian-born Brin, 30, is the son of a math professor and a scientist at NASA. The duo hatched a breakthrough search algorithm at a time when virtually everyone else considered Internet search a developer's cul de sac. Their next job, just as important, was to make their service lightning fast. The Google team pulled this off by stitching together some 10,000 servers and building, in effect, its own supercomputer. This jerry-rigged approach gave Google a sizable lead on the competition in both software and hardware. The pattern was set: while well-organized foes would wring revenues from the tried-and-true, Google's unbridled engineers would blaze new trails.

Page and Brin's radical management philosophy is derived from their experiences in the labs of Stanford University's computer science program. Google's managers rarely tell engineers what projects to tackle. Instead, executives keep a "Top 100" priorities list (which today contains more than 240 items), and engineers gravitate to issues that interest them, forming fluid working groups that can last for weeks or months. Engineers are urged to spend about one day a week working on their own personal research projects, no matter how offbeat, in hopes of sparking the Next Big Thing. "We're encouraging creativity and tolerating chaos," says Wayne Rosing, Google's vice president for engineering. "We turn that dial all the way over to loud."

Google coddles even its engineers' zaniest ideas. In one project, techies were grappling with the problem of displaying information from the Internet on cell phone screens, recalls a former Google employee. They went as far as pondering a laser that would scan the user's retina, creating the appearance of a larger screen. Ideas such as these are often included on the Top 100 list. An "S" next to a project stands for "skunkworks" and protects that project from premature reviews and criticism.

To foster a culture of creativity, the company's campus is a veritable theme park for propeller heads. Engineers unwind by playing roller hockey in the downstairs garage or racing remote-control blimps through the offices. Segway scooters, which retail at $4,000, are parked around campus, offering a novel way to navigate between buildings. Perks are lavish, from two flat-screen monitors on each computer to $800 digital toilets, equipped with remote controls to adjust seat temperature and water pressure.

POWER MOVE

Often entrepreneurs find it difficult to give up control when they bring in outsiders. But Page and Brin understood their strengths and weaknesses and turned over day-to-day management to Schmidt.

Brin and Page have been searching for the right mix of freedom and discipline for years. Back in 2000, the cofounders first hunkered down with Schmidt, then CEO of corporate software maker Novell Inc. Schmidt, a veteran of the software industry with the bruises to show for it, was taking a thrashing at the hands of Microsoft. Earlier, he had weathered similar ordeals as a top executive at Sun Microsystems Inc. He was not considered a remarkable visionary, but that was one area where

Page and Brin didn't need help. What they were looking for was a grown-up manager, someone who could turn Google into a real business, much the way Tim Koogle had taken over from Yahoo's young founders five years earlier.

The conversation naturally turned to technology. Almost immediately, Schmidt found himself in an argument that dragged on for most of the 90-minute meeting. Page and Brin were curt and headstrong, but Schmidt was impressed by their intelligence and passion. He left the meeting intrigued. Schmidt watched the company grow, and the next year he took over, first as chairman and four months later as CEO.

POWER MOVE

When it comes to technology, consumers want things kept simple. Google's search engine has remained popular, in part, because it keeps its home page uncluttered and provides fast, reliable search results.

"IT'S JUST BRUTAL"

Google finally had its grown-up. Page, who had been CEO, stepped down to president for products. Brin, formerly chairman, shifted to president for technology. Yet Schmidt, in his three-year tenure, has left the management structure intact. And the two founders aren't shy about flexing their muscles. "We've actually had a number of initiatives—I'd rather not go into specifics—where somebody, usually Larry or Sergey, says, 'Look, this thing's just not good enough.' And it's just brutal," Schmidt concedes.

To their credit, Page and Brin have made a string of inspired strategic moves that would make even the boldest tycoon blush with envy. They have steadfastly refused to clutter the home page with splashy ads or links to other Web sites, maintaining a zippy, minimalist design that has scarcely changed to this day. They scorned the marketing mania of the Internet boom, killing a multimillion-dollar advertising plan in 1999 and relying instead on word of mouth to build their hip and innovative brand. They built a business out of selling paid ads alongside search results, which turned Google into a money machine. Most important, they provided fast and reliable results, propelling Google from handling less than 1 percent of Web searches in 2000 to handling over 50 percent today.

Yet Google's rivals enjoy key advantages beyond search. Yahoo, for example, has proved adroit at wringing cash out of its site, particularly since the 2001 arrival of Semel. It has built a substantial retail business by catering to its regular users. It maintains profiles of shoppers, including delivery and credit card information. Yahoo also provides a universal shopping cart, letting a shopper store, say, a new blender from one retailer while exploring elsewhere for just the right gift. The result: shoppers can save a good 10 to 15 minutes each shopping session, compared with Google's price-comparison engine, dubbed Froogle, which can't store profiles or provide a digital cart. While 30,000 merchants pay $50 or more each month to be part of Yahoo's shopping network, Google has no comparable business.

Semel & Co. also have pushed aggressively to generate more money from search. Yahoo has embraced a practice known as "paid inclusion," in which a search engine accepts payment from a company to guarantee that the company's site is included somewhere in relevant search results. Often, the listing is not marked as advertising. This is big business; it's expected to grow from $200 million last year to $600 million in 2007, according to Piper Jaffray. But not one penny of this goes to Google. Why? Google decries paid inclusion as a blemish on the integrity of search results. It separates and clearly marks as advertising all links for which it's being paid.

> **POWER MOVE**
>
> Google understands that for a product to "scale," or reach a wide market, it must offer more than just a cool new technology. It has to provide a solution to a problem that many consumers face.

COURTING TRUST

This tussle over paid inclusion exposes a strategic rift. Google is sticking to its position that search is an editorial product, with a clear line between information and ads. The bet is that this stance will foster public trust in the brand and pay off with increased traffic to the site. But if the public does not focus on ad policies, Google's foes stand to mine a rich new market—perhaps pressuring Google to follow suit. Fredrick Marckini, CEO of search marketing firm iProspect, says: "People tend not to notice [paid inclusions]." This may lead Google executives to launch a PR campaign on the issue. "It's something we debate," says Page.

For now, Google is battling Yahoo with innovations such as Gmail. The strategy extends far beyond luring people to the site with free e-mail. It opens up vast new terrain for Google to search. It won't be long, for instance, before Gmail users can toggle between searching the Web and their archived e-mails with a single click. Eventually, Google could tap data such as zip code and gender from these profiles to better compete head-to-head with Yahoo in customized search. "The more information we have when we do a search, the better it's going to work," says Page.

POWER MOVE

Google maintains customer loyalty by protecting the integrity of its brand—even if that means lower short-term profits. So while other search engines have increased revenue by including companies in their search results in exchange for a fee, Google has steadfastly refused to follow suit.

An advertising bonanza is at stake. For now, Google is the leader in paid search, a market that is expected to grow from $2 billion last year to $4.8 billion in 2005, says Deutsche Bank Securities Inc. But future growth hinges on customization. Already, Yahoo and AOL are exploring ways to customize searches for willing visitors based on data that they have stored in profiles. "You don't have to plug [the zip code] in," says Gerry Campbell, vice president of AOL Search. "It can be pulled right from your profile." Google offers a service that lets people enter their location and contends that having the information stored isn't much of an advantage. After all, people may be searching for a restaurant when they're away from home on a business trip. Even if they're at home, Page says, it's simple to type in the five-digit code.

In time, search engines will feast on every bit of personal information we're willing to share, and will serve up links that fit our tastes and locales—maybe even fine-tuning them according to the time of day. It's a market that's headed for dramatic growth and change. No wonder so many investors are grasping for a piece of the brand that has become synonymous with search. "Google represents the new era," says Michael Moe, chief executive of boutique investment bank ThinkEquity Partners. But buyers beware: Google's biggest tests are dead ahead.

MONDAY MORNING...

THE PROBLEM

Maintaining market leadership in an industry that is crowded with large, aggressive competitors

Forging a close working partnership between the founders and the CEO, so that the company operates smoothly and avoids conflicts

Creating a culture of creativity so that the company continues to release cutting-edge products

THE SOLUTION

Aim for mass appeal by continuing to develop new technology that will offer solutions to people's most common problems.

Ensure that the company founders understand their weaknesses as well as their strengths, so that they're willing to cede control to others when necessary.

Avoid power struggles by putting one person in charge of day-to-day management, someone who is comfortable collaborating with the founders when making major decisions.

Empower employees at all levels of the company by giving them the opportunity to pursue new, unorthodox ideas.

SUSTAINING THE WIN

Stay focused on the company's mission, making sure that new products and initiatives serve long-term objectives.

SERGEY BRIN and LARRY PAGE

GREG NORMAN:
ALL BUSINESS

POWER PLAYER

Greg Norman's empire runs the gamut from golf course design to wine. His businesses generate more than $300 million in annual revenues. How did he do it? By taking the long view and protecting his brand image, he's been able to take control of his own money and his destiny.

This 2005 profile by Dean Foust takes an in-depth look at an athlete who has transcended his sport.

LESSON PLAN

Create and maintain a quality brand by being very choosy, undertaking only ventures that will enhance your good name.

Remain knowledgeable about and actively involved in your businesses in order to ensure that your cadre of managers, agents, and others are running them effectively.

Avoid major missteps by studying and learning from others' mistakes, as well as from your own.

PRO GOLFER AND ENTREPRENEUR

It's a steamy summer morning, and Greg Norman is itching to play golf. After back pain forced him to withdraw from the PGA Championship in mid-August, Norman is eager to walk 18 holes at the Medalist Golf Club near his Jupiter Island (Florida) home to see if he has recovered sufficiently to compete in the Jeld-Wen Tradition Champions Tour tournament in Aloha, Oregon, the next week.

But the round is full of interruptions—the kind that any golf-playing CEO would appreciate. As Norman approaches the twelfth hole, his cell phone rings; it's a call from Reebok International CEO Paul Fireman. Norman retreats to the shade and spends 20 minutes discussing Adidas-Salomon's pending buyout of Reebok—specifically, how it might affect the Greg Norman clothing line that Reebok produces. On the next hole, Bart Collins—who oversees the day-to-day affairs of Norman's myriad business ventures—zooms up in a cart and pulls his boss aside for an impromptu meeting.

After he putts out on number 18, Norman can banish any thoughts of hitting a few more balls on the range. Instead, he heads directly to the clubhouse dining room, where a wine company executive is waiting to give him a final tasting of the new line of Greg Norman California wines that will hit retail shelves in the fall. After Norman murmurs his approval of the five varietals he's given to taste, he dashes off to dinner with the ghostwriter of a Simon & Schuster book he's working on for release next June. A golf instruction guide? That was the old Norman. In this book, Norman plans to offer management tips based on his experiences as a pro golfer and entrepreneur.

Despite winning 86 tournaments over his 29-year pro golf career, Norman may never shake the images of his collapse in the 1996 Masters, where he blew a six-stroke lead and lost to Nick Faldo by five strokes, or his failure to win more majors than his two British Opens. But in the business arena, Norman has achieved a level of success matched by few other golfers. As head of Great White Shark Enterprises Inc., Norman presides over a sprawling empire that spans everything from golf course design to winemaking to turf grass.

MORE HITS THAN MISSES

Norman's apparel line, the Greg Norman Collection, rings up nearly $200 million in annual retail sales, making it one of the most popular clothing lines endorsed by any athlete. His Greg Norman Estates, a six-year-old joint venture with Foster's Wine Estates, now sells 230,000 cases of Australian wine a year—a strong performance that has inspired Foster's to launch California wines under the Norman label as well. Medallist Developments, a joint venture between Norman and Macquarie Bank Ltd. of Australia, currently has more than 10,000 golf course homes under construction in the United States, Mexico, and Australia and is mulling an expansion to other parts of the globe. Setbacks—such as a Greg Norman–themed restaurant and a Paul Newman–like line of foods—have been relatively rare.

Norman's payoff has been huge. While he claims that he was "virtually broke" early in his playing career, Norman, 50, now oversees a business empire generating more than $300 million in annual revenues. Although he's more than a decade past his playing prime, Norman still exudes a magnetism that appeals even to consumers who have never picked up a golf club. "Norman has done what few athletes are able to do, to transcend his sport," says Eldon Ham, an adjunct professor of sports and law at the Chicago-Kent College of Law. "There's a little Crocodile Dundee in him, and in marketing, attitude is one of the traits you're selling."

It has been quite an odyssey for Norman, who as a young tour pro showed little interest in business matters. In *Shark: The Biography of Greg Norman*, author Lauren St. John writes that a

POWER MOVE

When it comes to building a business, charisma counts. Even consumers who have little interest in golf are drawn to products hawked by the appealing Greg Norman, a golf legend turned mega-entrepreneur with clothing, wine, and golf course design ventures.

younger Norman sometimes fell asleep in meetings with prospective business partners—"bored rigid by the plotting and planning he paid others to do." He took an interest only after a couple of deals went awry. (Norman takes issue with this characterization.) As he began to win tournaments, he admits that he paid a price for not paying closer attention to how other people handled his affairs. "Typical athlete, I got f---ed over by my agent and found myself in trouble with the Australian taxation office," he says. "But I learned an important lesson: take control over your own money, your own destiny."

POWER MOVE

It's fine to delegate, but if you don't stay well informed, especially about your financial matters, you put yourself at risk. Norman claims that he was "virtually broke" early on because he ceded control to others and didn't keep tabs on them. Now he is involved in all aspects of his businesses, from long-term planning to new designs for his clothing line.

After signing with über-agency IMG in the 1980s, Norman grew dissatisfied with the hefty fees—10 percent of his winnings and 25 percent of merchandising income—and what he felt was IMG's fast-buck mentality. "They don't take the long view because they're only working on a three- or five-year contract, and there's always another star right behind you," he says. "I didn't want to be playing golf beyond 65 because I had to." Tensions came to a head in 1993 when IMG demanded a cut of the $44 million Norman reaped as an early investor in clubmaker Cobra Golf after its sale to American Brands—a deal that Norman insists he'd negotiated himself.

GOING IT ALONE

So in the early 1990s, Norman, his popularity soaring, chose not to renew his contract with IMG and began managing his own affairs. Known for being hard on caddies, swing coaches, and disruptive galleries, he proved to be just as tough as a businessman: Biographer St. John notes that Norman could be stinting with his praise and once didn't speak with his former top executive, Frank Williams, for three months during a tiff.

(Collins says Norman has mellowed.) Some business partners say that Norman can be just as exacting with them. "He's incredibly demanding," says Fireman. "He demands great product and innovation." But the Reebok CEO gives him credit for thrusting himself deeper into decision making than most athletes—everything from approving potential clothing designs to long-term strategy. "He truly wants to build his brand for the long term, and that's a big difference from most athletes," Fireman says.

Over time, Norman says, he has made a point of studying—and learning from—the mistakes of other pro golfers–turned-businessmen. For example, Norman believes that Arnold Palmer may have cheapened his image by being too indiscriminate with his endorsements. "I could have endorsed car washes and underwear, but things like that don't build up your brand," he says. After studying Jack Nicklaus's well-publicized problems—a soured real estate venture left Nicklaus financially overextended in the mid-1980s—Norman decided to sharply limit how much of his own money he put into deals. "Jack was a strong enough brand that he did not need to put his own neck on the line," he says. In both his real estate venture with Macquarie Bank and his winemaking partnership with Foster's, Norman put up not a cent—and received a 30 percent equity stake in each just for lending his name and image. Late last year, MacGregor Golf sweetened its deal for Norman to promote its new Mactec driver and other golf clubs by giving the Shark stock options on top of his endorsement fee, says MacGregor CEO Barry Schneider.

Still, not all of Norman's ventures have panned out. In Australia, he scrapped plans to introduce a line of pasta sauces

POWER MOVE

Many top executives and entrepreneurs say that they've made a point of learning from their failures. Norman has gone even further, studying his peers' mistakes. Believing that Arnold Palmer may have weakened his name by endorsing too many products, for instance, Norman has been far more selective. He has turned down deals because they would dilute his brand.

POWER MOVE

Norman limits his financial risks by not investing much of his own money in new ventures. He understands that his brand is a powerful enough asset that he can attract partners by lending his name, not his money.

and other foods after the products generated mixed results in test markets. Collins says that the food line was designed to be nothing more than a charitable venture à la Paul Newman, but "the message that it was cause-related never got through."

While Norman joined with restaurateur Todd English to create six Greg Norman's Australian Grille restaurants, only one—the original, in North Myrtle Beach, South Carolina— has opened. Collins acknowledges that Norman chose the wrong partner for the restaurant, which bled red ink from the beginning. But under a new management team, the restaurant has managed to turn a profit in each of the past two years, and Collins says that Great White Shark Enterprises is planning to seek a major restaurant chain to expand the Australian Grille concept to other markets.

While the demand for Norman's golf course design services remains strong, critics contend that his record as a course architect is mixed. Despite charging a relatively hefty $1.25 million design fee, Norman says that he currently has about three dozen courses in some phase of development—a strong showing at a time when many other architects are scratching for business. To his credit, *Golf Digest* named his Doonbeg Golf Club, located on Ireland's rugged western coast, the "Best New International Course" in 2002. In the United States, *Golf Digest* has put at least three Norman designs—Shark's Tooth in Lake Powell, Florida, TPC at Sugarloaf in Atlanta, and the Reserve in Pawleys Island, South Carolina— on its best new course lists over the past decade.

But Norman has also seen two courses he built reworked or bulldozed by developers who deemed his layouts too challenging for average golfers. That was the case in Scottsdale, Arizona, where he designed a resort course known as Stonehaven for Lehman Brothers Inc. After Lehman sold the

development to Discovery Land Co. of San Francisco—
which immediately converted it to a private club—Discovery
determined that the design was too demanding for its members.
"We saw the course as not being playable enough, so we tore
it up and started from scratch," says Discovery partner Steve
Adelson. While the Norman layout had a mere 42 acres of
fairway—meaning that most wayward shots ended up in the
desert—architect Tom Fazio created a much more forgiving
90-acre tract.

Such setbacks have been the exception throughout
Norman's career as a businessman. He says his ultimate goal
is to emulate the success of René Lacoste, a tennis
star–turned–clothing designer from the 1930s whose legacy is
the ubiquitous alligator logo. "Not many people know him for
what he was—a good tennis player, not a great tennis player,"
says Norman. "But he created a brand that lives on. That's what
you want to do, to leave a legacy, a trust in perpetuity for your
children." Norman hopes that will be his final conquest.

THE PROBLEM
Parlaying huge success in one profession into a multifaceted business empire

Developing and launching new, ambitious ventures without becoming financially overextended

THE SOLUTION
Leverage your image and your reputation for excellence. Negotiate for equity stakes in exchange for lending your name—not your money—to new companies.

Use your natural charm and star power to win over consumers and partners.

Recognize that you don't need to be an expert to branch out into new, unfamiliar industries—if you partner with worthy, competent professionals and monitor them closely.

SUSTAINING THE WIN
Continue to expand into new areas, but do so cautiously, turning down even lucrative offers if they might tarnish your brand.

GREG NORMAN

JOHNATHAN WENDEL:
CAN PRO GAMING GO LEGIT?

POWER PLAYER

With his success and good looks, Johnathan Wendel is popularizing pro gaming around the world. Wendel aims to turn this niche phenomenon into a popular sport that is watched by millions on the Internet and on television.

This 2005 special report by Steve Hamm, with Beth Carney, profiles Wendel and the world of pro gaming. Also included is Steve Hamm's news analysis of the finale of the Cyberathlete Pro League World Tour.

LESSON PLAN

Aggressively pursue and believe in your ambitions, even if the field is nascent and not yet recognized by others.

Make sure to branch out into new platforms. Form relationships and partnerships with companies that can offer new revenue streams and help build your brand.

Remain committed to being the best. Use a loss to propel you to work harder so that you win the next time.

Be prepared for tough new competitors who will challenge the status quo as the industry matures and grows.

CAN JOHNATHAN "FATAL1TY" WENDEL WIN
CREDIBILITY FOR PRO GAMING—AND FOR HIMSELF?

Rock music blares. Spotlights slice through the air. Young men in black T-shirts chatter excitedly. It's September 3, Sheffield, Britain. The Cyberathlete Professional League tournament has taken over a sprawling former steel mill in this city north of London. One competitor stands out: Johnathan "Fatal1ty" Wendel. He clamps a headset into his ears, using the techno music to isolate himself from the crowd. The tall, blond 24-year-old is America's most successful gamer, and here he's all business. He's determined to take down archrival Sander "VoO" Kaasjager, a 20-year-old Dutchman who has dominated the CPL all year. Wendel trounced Kaasjager in the previous tournament, in Dallas, in July, and he means to do it again.

Before he gets to Kaasjager, though, Wendel will face off against Alexander "Ztrider" Ingarv. The 18-year-old Swede finished third in Dallas and is always a threat. Wendel takes his position at a PC on one of a string of tables lined up along a wall—with Ingarv sitting a few chairs away. On their screens: the interior of a gloomy castle where their two characters will pursue each other at dizzying speeds through a labyrinth of rooms and blast away when they make contact. The game is *Painkiller*, and in this tournament version, the characters are "brightskins"—red silhouettes of men that stand out as targets. The player who kills his opponent the most times in 15 minutes is the winner. It's a best-of-three match.

Ingarv gets off to a fast start. He fires away and gets a couple of quick kills. A few minutes into the match, Wendel starts clawing back. He has a knack for counting the seconds until a weapon, ammo, or armor will materialize at a particular spot in the maze and being there to claim it. Cheers and jeers erupt as Wendel takes the lead. When time runs out, he wins in a squeaker, 16 to 15.

The second game is no contest: after five minutes, Ingarv is shaking his head dejectedly. As the thrashing grows more one-sided, a small crowd that had gathered around Wendel grows quiet. The final game's score: 31 to 7.

What's all the hubbub about? Unbeknownst to almost everyone over 30, professional game playing is becoming a very big deal. There are worldwide tours with stops from Rio de Janeiro to Istanbul. Celebrity players are hounded for autographs and compete for high-stakes prizes. At the CPL World Tour Grand Finals in New York in November, players will compete for a total of $500,000 in cash.

CYBERSPACE STATESMAN

In this new world, Johnathan Wendel is the undisputed star. Over a period of five years, he has won more tournaments and pulled in more prize money than any other player, a total that has now topped $350,000. Girl gamers buzz about him at matches, like a group of Swedish players in Barcelona this summer. And boys idolize him. "He's so good," says Iisakki "Beam" Ahonen, an up-and-coming 17-year-old Finn player. "I want to be like him—to travel and compete in tournaments and make a living at it."

Yet Wendel is doing far more than just winning tournaments. He has become one of the key figures in popularizing computer games throughout the world. With his success and his clean-cut good looks, he plays the role of statesman for his sport, the Tiger Woods or Michael Jordan of cyberspace. He aspires to help turn a niche phenomenon into a popular sport watched by millions of fans on TV and the Internet. "I want to bring gaming mainstream, "Wendel says.

POWER MOVE

Creating a viable business in an industry that is in its infancy requires guts and tenacity. Ignoring the skeptics and naysayers, Johnathan "Fatal1ty" Wendel relentlessly pursued his passion, even when gaming was derided as a fringe hobby for geeks. Now he is the top-earning gamer.

If Wendel's hand-eye coordination is admirable, his market timing may be even better. Electronic gaming is exploding and spreading everywhere—from consoles and PCs to online communities and cell phones. More than 300 million people play worldwide, fueling an industry that is expected to rake in $34 billion in revenues this year, according to market researcher DFC Intelligence. Worldwide box-office receipts for movies, in comparison, were $21.4 billion last year.

That has pro gaming at the tipping point. Webcasts of the tournaments have grown increasingly popular, with 25 being shown this year, up from 2 in 2000. Traditional TV producers are getting on board. In November, ESPN plans on broadcasting an eight-part documentary about a team that plays the game *John Madden NFL Football*. MTV Networks will cover action from the CPL finals in New York. And HDNet, the high-definition TV network, is scoping out tournament coverage. "Watching the teams go at it, the battles are incredibly competitive," says Mark Cuban, cofounder of HDNet and owner of the NBA's Dallas Mavericks.

Wendel may be just the sort of bona fide superstar to push gaming over the top. He's six feet tall, slim, and athletic. "The gamer image is out-of-shape, pasty, nerdy, smelly," says Roger L. Kay, president of tech market research outfit Endpoint Technologies Associates. "This guy can promote the industry as a cool place to be."

But Johnathan Wendel is a different sort of star from Tiger or Michael. His game takes place in another dimension: the emerging realm of cyberspace. In a sense, he's a guide to the future. For his generation, the Internet is the sandlot baseball diamond, Main Street, and the neighborhood cinema all rolled into one. Online, its members play

POWER MOVE

Early entrants into any field have to be prepared for fierce competition down the road. When the field explodes in popularity, it inevitably attracts more formidable competitors. When Wendell first turned pro in 1999, there were just a handful of top players. Now there are two dozen.

games, instant message, and share their lives with people halfway around the world.

To win these people over, media and entertainment businesses have to learn to play by new rules. And to market to this key demographic, companies from Ford Motor Co. to Procter & Gamble Co. have to get with it, too. They all need to recognize that the Web is evolving into a global forum for sport, communications, and entertainment. In cyberspace, Wendel is as much Tom Cruise as Tiger Woods. "Traditional businesses need to plug in," says Saul J. Berman, a consultant in IBM's entertainment industry practice. "This is the consumer base of the future. Somebody who doesn't understand this stuff won't be able to spot the opportunities and the threats."

Certainly, many companies are beginning to see opportunity in gaming. News Corp., for instance, just paid $650 million for game-site operator IGN Entertainment Inc. Big-name tech companies Intel Corp. and Samsung Group are putting up the prize money for many of the tournaments worldwide. They hope to benefit from the halo effect of being associated with the coolest, fastest gamers and sell more high-end gear. The average desktop PC price is about $800 compared to $3,000 for a jazzed-up gamer PC. But interest in gaming goes well beyond techies. Consumer-products companies are sponsoring gamers, too. Tylenol backs Team Ouch!

The biggest prize may go to Wendel himself. He's working to establish a worldwide brand, something that no gamer has ever done. He's licensing the Fatal1ty name (pronounced simply "fatality") to several hardware makers and expects to come out with a Fatal1ty PC soon. Down the line, he'll introduce hats, clothing, and even static-resistant shoes. "He's beyond games. He's the spokesperson for the digital revolution," says Mark Walden, director of licensing at Auravision Inc. in Woodland Hills, California, Wendel's master licenser.

Yet for Wendel, this quest is about much more than building his own business. Strip away all the trappings, and what he's doing is shooting for respect. As a hard-core gamer,

POWER MOVE

Wendel's intense drive to win has been critical to his success. "Johnathan doesn't like to lose. He thinks he should win all the time," says his father, James. "Being number one shows your character and your will," Wendel says.

he's a member of a clan of outcasts—the people who didn't quite fit in. Now the crazy tech stuff they're good at is cool. So Wendel is out to prove that PC gaming is legit—not only to the world, but also to his own mother. After his parents divorced when he was 13, his mother cracked down on his game playing. They fought so bitterly that he left home for good on the eve of his high school graduation. "This is about proving her wrong," Wendel says. "She never believed in me. The day I drive up in front of her door in a Ferrari is the day I close the door on that subject."

But if Wendel is to achieve his goals, he has to keep winning, and this has been a tough year. Wendel placed fourth and sixth in early tilts before rising to second and finally taking first place in July. The pressure is on for him to win the CPL championship in New York. "You've got to win. You can't just be around, not winning. Young kids want to emulate the best of the best of the best," says Mike Antinoro, executive producer of ESPN Original Entertainment, creator of the *Madden* series.

Back in Sheffield, it's the last day of the three-day tourney. Fatal1ty and VoO breezed through the preliminaries. Now, they're playing each other. The one who wins this best-of-three match will go straight to the finals, while the other one will have to fight through other contenders to earn a spot.

The two don't make eye contact before the bout. Wendel settles down at a PC at one end of the string of tables. Kaasjager is sitting a few seats away, but out of sight. In the first game of the match, Fatal1ty easily beats VoO, 32 to 12. He studies his opponents to anticipate their moves, and he mixes up his own style so he's unpredictable.

The second game is a nail-biter. They trade kill for kill. Kaasjager yells at the screen in Dutch. Wendel is mum until the end. When he wins by a point, 16 to 15, he yells "Yeah!" and pumps his fist before threading through the crowd and perfunctorily shaking Kaasjager's hand. "That was awesome," he says. "That was the biggest match, right there."

Victories like that don't come easy. When Wendel first turned pro, back in 1999, there were only a handful of worthy opponents. Now there are two dozen elite players. To stay on top of his game, he practices tirelessly. Between tournament appearances and promotional "Fatal1ty Shootouts" at trade shows, he'll duck out for a few hours and practice in his hotel room. He even has a sparring partner whom he takes on the road—Brian "Zen" Grapatin, a 23-year-old former club tennis pro.

But Wendel truly gets into the practice groove only when he's at home in Kansas City, Missouri. He rents a basement room in a modest ranch house off I-435. His roommate and longtime friend Jarod Reisin makes his living as a valet parking attendant at a local nightspot. Some of the decor is from the 1960s, with knotty pine paneling in the living room and, in the kitchen, turquoise kitchen countertops and mint-condition plastic-covered chairs. But most of the furnishings are pure 1990s—big cushy couches clustered around a five-foot TV, surround-sound speakers, and posters of Bruce Lee and *Star Wars*'s Yoda on the walls. When a reporter visited, Wendel whipped up his favorite snack, a dip of ground beef and melted Velveeta.

The basement is Fatal1ty's virtual workout gym. It's a large, dark room crowded with a huge waterbed, the headboard lined with gleaming trophies and gamer memorabilia.

POWER MOVE

In a youth-driven field, where it's possible to be over the hill at 30, the established pros have to work hard in order to stay at the top. Wendel is known for his fanatical devotion to his work, often putting in eight hours a day practicing.

In one corner there's a boxy *Mortal Kombat* arcade game. This was Wendel's first love. He took his gamer handle from the word that flashes on the screen at the end of a *Mortal Kombat* contest: Fatality! Four PCs are set up on tables and connected via a network. When Wendel is home, the day goes like this: up at noon, game, eat, run three miles, game, game some more, watch a movie, snack, game even more, and turn in at about 4 a.m. Altogether, he practices eight hours a day.

It's not easy being Fatal1ty's sparring partner. "When we started last year, I'd win 40 percent of the time. Now it's 10 percent," says Grapatin. "It's gotten to the point where I have trouble playing with him. He's on a whole other level." Fatal1ty brings in new players to compete with—and to give Zen a break. In August, he sent bus tickets to Kansas City to two gamers in Texas and Minnesota.

Late one night at Wendel's, Fatal1ty knocks the stuffing out of Zen in *Painkiller*. He stares intently at the computer screen as his character moves rapidly through the game set. His right hand, holding the mouse, sways gracefully from side to side. Suddenly, a red silhouette of a man hops out of nowhere and Fatal1ty blasts away, the fingers of his left hand tap dancing across the keyboard. Fatal1ty and Zen barely speak during the intense 15-minute session. The only sounds are the roar of guns and the grunts of monsters. Final score: 51–8. Just then, Reisin sidles down the stairs. "Who's winning?" he asks. Everybody laughs.

POWER MOVE

Wendel may well succeed in building a global brand. The reason: he recognized and seized the new market opportunities. Seeing that gaming was gaining mass appeal, he became the first gamer to ink a deal with a company to sell gear with his logo on it.

A TASTE OF SUCCESS

What makes Fatal1ty stand out from other top gamers? In addition to natural athletic ability and clever strategies, he works harder than many others. While they think of gaming as play, he considers it a full-time job—and puts in the commensurate hours. He also has some qualities that are hard to describe. After playing all of those hours and memorizing the look and feel of imaginary worlds, he gets into a zone, Zenlike, where much of what he does is instinctual. Then there's the X factor: an unquenchable thirst for winning.

None of this is accidental. Wendel grew up in a striving blue-collar household in the shadow of Kansas City's Royals' stadium. His parents worked in auto factories, and his father ran a pool hall on the side. A formative experience came when, at about age seven, young Johnathan fell while playing in a stream behind the pool hall and cut his wrist badly on some broken glass. A doctor recommended that he play sports to help complete his recovery. The kid obliged by mastering baseball, football, tennis, hockey, Ping-Pong, bowling, golf, and billiards. He takes play to an extreme. "Johnathan doesn't like to lose. He thinks he should win all the time," says his father, James. Wendel appreciates his dad: after he won $40,000 in a tournament in 2000, he plunked down $29,000 in cash and bought James a Cadillac.

With mom, it was different. His parents broke up as Wendel was entering adolescence. His father had bought Wendel and his younger sister and brother a Nintendo console and let them play games on his PC, but Judy Wendel thought electronic games were a waste of time. She and her new husband were disciplinarians, and according to Wendel and his sister, Jenny, they punished the kids frequently for breaking rules. "Over and over, he was grounded from playing on the computer—what he loved to do," says Jenny, 23, a college student. Wendel's mother wouldn't comment on past conflicts. "I love my son. Gaming is his life. I don't interfere," she says.

After graduating from high school, Wendel dreamed of going pro. He was living with his dad, taking computer classes, and working part-time. The night before his first big tournament, in Dallas in late 1999, his father came into his bedroom to talk to him about his future. "I told him I needed to go. I wanted my chance," recalls Wendel. "I told him if I didn't win money, I'd go to school full-time."

He never got back to the books. Wendel won a $550 prize, and a week later, he won again—this time $4,000. In no time, he was on the just-jelling pro circuit, playing tournaments in far-flung locales from Seoul and Melbourne to Cologne and Rio de Janeiro. "Right then, I set my goal. I wanted to be the number one player in the world," says Wendel. "I wanted to show my dominance, my skill. Being number one shows your character and your will. You get so much respect."

POWER MOVE

Wendel has a keen understanding of his industry and is focusing on creating products that amateur and pro gamers will both want. So he is involved with products ranging from a bigger-than-usual mouse pad to high-performance accelerator cards and cooling fans—all with his logo on them.

MAKING HIS MARQUE

All the travel is a blast for Wendel and his pals. They often jet around together, and they make videos of their exploits. Once they flew into Turkey in shorts and T-shirts, only to find a blizzard raging at the airport. At a Korean hotel, 30 people got into a cake fight in a hallway. They're supposed to go on a safari next week in South Africa. "We're walking around some weird country doing whatever we want," says Grapatin. "It's starting to get normal—which is weird in itself."

Over time, Fatal1ty the ace gamer and good-timer morphed into Fatal1ty the businessman. At first it was simple stuff. He designed a bigger-than-usual mouse pad featuring the Fatal1ty logo and started selling the pads online. But last year things got a lot more serious. He knew he could remain a top player for only so long, so he needed to build something more enduring than a winning streak. He became the first—and so far the only—gamer to get hardware makers to design products with his logo on them. His first partner was ABIT Computer Corp., a Taiwanese maker of PC motherboards and graphics cards. Next came Zalman, a maker of PC cooling fans—a must for gamers, who tweak their processors to run fast and hot—and Creative Labs, a leading maker of PC sound cards and MP3 players.

Balancing business with gaming has proven tricky, however. It's VoO, not Fatal1ty, who's tearing up the pro circuit this year. There's no love lost between these two. Kaasjager admits he doesn't have much use for Wendel. "What can be quite annoying is he gets all the attention—much more than me," he says.

Over the summer, Wendel put more time into practice, and by the time of the Dallas tilt in July, he was in top form. And the rivalry was fiercer than ever. Just before the finals, he returned to his computer to find Kaasjager sitting at his keyboard, fondling his lucky stuffed tiger, smU. Wendel shouted for Kaasjager to keep his hands off his stuff. "It was like somebody playing with Tiger Woods's putter. I went ballistic," Wendel recalls. He calmed down, though, and beat VoO resoundingly.

POWER MOVE

Like many people who become celebrities (and build popular brands), Wendel is skilled at self-promotion. Tall and good-looking, with an ability to tell his "story" in an engaging way, he has become a media favorite and is the star of the industry.

In Sheffield, after his defeat by Fatal1ty, VoO wins match after match. Ultimately, he fights his way into the finals, and the two archrivals face off on a brightly lit stage. The action is projected on giant screens above their heads. A crowd of about 70 gathers around the stage and cheers them on, while thousands more tune in via a live Webcast from Team Sportscast Network LLC. TSN "shoutcasters" call the play-by-play. Fatal1ty has an edge; he won their previous match. Now, he has to win only one best-of-three match, while VoO needs two matches in a row.

Yet Fatal1ty falters. The first game is close, but VoO triumphs, 22 to 20. In the second game, VoO wins 29 to 16. Fatal1ty is visibly frustrated, shaking his head as he plays. The first match is VoO's. After losing a third game, 33 to 16, he asks to have his PC changed, and officials spend 20 minutes replacing it, which doesn't help. VoO wins the final game in a rout, 17 to 9. When time runs out, VoO yells "Yes!" and Fatal1ty stands up, takes a deep breath, and shakes his head. "I played bad," he says. He thinks he may have overpracticed during the long delays before the finals and tired himself out: "I'll be better prepared next time."

He'd better. The next big tournament comes at the CPL championship in New York City. His backers make light of the situation. "Even Michael Jordan misses a shot sometimes," says Lester Lau, gamer branding manager at ABIT. But, the truth is, the pressure is on. "The young guys are coming up, and they're going to be challenging some of these old dinosaurs like Johnathan," says Sheryl Huang, a marketing manager for NVIDIA Corp., a maker of chips for gaming peripherals.

Could Wendel be over the hill at 24? In this game, it's possible. He's keenly aware of the risks. "I'll have to peak again for this event," he says. Later, in an e-mail, he adds: "Now my goal is to move onto the next big game (next year) and become world champion at another game. But, before I give *Painkiller* a rest, I would definitely like to go out on top in November."

Going out on top has a nice ring to it. And, for Wendel, it would be especially gratifying. He has worked hard for five years to build his skills, his brand, and his sport. Now comes his big chance to show the world—and his mom—that he and his game deserve their respect.

NEWS ANALYSIS: PRO GAMING LIVES LARGE

A championship in Times Square marks a coming of age for video gaming—and a springboard to the big time for Johnathan "Fatal1ty" Wendel.

The finale of the Cyberathlete Professional League 2005 world tour on November 22 could have been scripted in Hollywood. Facing off were Sander "VoO" Kaasjager, the 20-year-old Dutchman who had dominated the CPL's one-on-one competitions this year, vs. Johnathan "Fatal1ty" Wendel, a 24-year-old from Kansas City who is computer gaming's perennial champion. The announcer called it "the biggest rivalry in computer gaming history." That was no exaggeration.

The setting was the Nokia Theater in New York's Times Square. The two combatants sat opposite each other at PCs on a stage. They jousted at *Painkiller*, an ultrafast shoot-'em-up that involves the taking of many virtual lives.

VoO had won five tournaments during the year, compared with just two for Fatal1ty. But VoO was no match for the veteran. Employing a devastating strategy of first hiding out and then attacking aggressively, Fatal1ty won four games in a row and took the $150,000 prize.

SEDENTARY SPORT

VoO, with a baby face and a halo of buzz-cut blonde hair, was downcast. "I couldn't get my game going," he said afterward. "It was probably the most boring match in the history of *Painkiller*, but he won."

Fatal1ty, a tall, slim redhead, was delirious in victory. He posed holding a giant cardboard check while surrounded by seven beautiful young women dressed all in black. When asked what he would do with the paycheck, he was ready: "I'm going to take all my friends to spring break next year."

Amid the hoopla and youthful enthusiasm, the event was something of a coming of age for pro gaming. Born a decade ago in a Dallas hotel, the CPL tournament had finally made it to the big time—New York City. MTV was broadcasting the event live. A scrum of other camera crews crowded around. Thousands of kids compete in tournaments like this one all over the world, and tens of thousands vie for gaming glory online. Gaming has become a bona fide sport.

The CPL championship also served as an apt launchpad for the next phase of Wendel's career. While he plans to keep competing next year, he has a business on the side—think of it as Fatal1ty Inc.—that's just now taking off. Already he has licensed his brand for use with PC cards and cooling fans, and Fatal1ty keyboards and mice are due out next year.

NONVIRTUAL CASH

Mark Walden, director of licensing at Auravision in Woodland Hills, California, Wendel's master licenser, says partner Creative Labs is selling Fatal1ty sound cards at a clip of 30,000 a month. Wendel's already-high profile is about to get a bit higher, too. CBS plans to run a 15-minute segment on him on *60 Minutes* in December, and negotiations are under way with Random House for a book.

Wendel's tournament winnings alone have made him rich by kid standards—he has scooped up more than $500,000 in prize money over the past five years. And while Wendel basks in glory, don't feel sorry for Kaasjager. Even in defeat, he made out well. His $100,000 runner-up check, plus $20,000 for winning the most points during the tournament, bring his 2005 winnings to $240,000.

THE PROBLEM

Achieving mainstream popularity, respect, and success in a field that has been considered a quirky sideline

Maintaining dominance in an industry flooded with ever younger, stronger talent

THE SOLUTION

Set high goals and work obsessively to achieve them.

Court the media, so that you become a spokesperson for the industry and a celebrity.

Put in long hours practicing your craft and developing your skills.

Pay close attention to long-term trends so that you can jump on new market opportunities before your rivals do.

SUSTAINING THE WIN

Continue to grow your brand by using your sophisticated understanding of the industry to develop new products and services that consumers want.

JOHNATHAN
WENDEL

KEVIN ROSE: DIGG.COM'S NEW SILICON VALLEY BRAT PACK

POWER PLAYER

Kevin Rose's own biography on Digg.com reads, "An obsessive tea drinker, spends his time in between podcasting, climbing, digging, and inventing Digg's next gen features." Having witnessed the dot-com implosion of 2000, Rose and company are determined to stay on top.

This 2006 cover story by Sarah Lacy and Jessi Hempel profiles Digg.com founder Kevin Rose and his "Valley Boys."

Pour energy into developing a great business idea first, rather than raising lots of capital. Successful companies can now be launched on the Web with minimal seed money.

Work fast, bringing new products to market quickly and constantly in order to stay ahead of competitors.

Be selective when bringing in investors, making sure that you're not giving up decision making in exchange for cash that you might not need.

Listen to your gut rather than to focus groups and consultants. If you think a product would be enormously useful to you, it probably will be to others.

A NEW BRAT PACK OF YOUNG ENTREPRENEURS

It was 4:45 a.m. on June 26, and Digg founder Kevin Rose was slugging back tea and trying to keep his eyes open as he drove his Volkswagen Golf to Digg's headquarters above the offices of the *SF Bay Guardian* in Potrero Hill. This was the day Rose would test everything. Two years earlier, Rose had gambled on his idea for changing news gathering, letting the masses "dig up" the most interesting stories on the Web and vote them onto his online "front page" on Digg.com. Rose had given every last piece of himself to the project—all his time, all his cash, and even his girlfriend, who fought with him after he poured his savings into Digg instead of making a down payment on a house. Today, Digg, Version 3, the one that would go beyond tech news to include politics, gossip, business, and videos, was going live. At 29, Rose was on his way either to a cool $60 million or to total failure.

As Rose sat in the middle of the office, managing a final countdown, a Puma cap yanked over his eyes, his posse of 20- and 30-something engineers sat at their desks with contingency plans and extra servers ready. They flipped the switch. Stories started trickling in. The pace picked up, and suddenly it was a deluge. Digg staffers grew frenzied, screaming at one other to stay one step ahead of the traffic. By 4 p.m. on launch day, the site had signed up more than 13,000 new registered users, eight times the average number. Traffic was clocking in at four times the volume of the previous Monday. The news of Digg's launch was lighting up the blogosphere. An exhausted Rose collapsed for a snooze under his desk.

POWER MOVE

Rose, like many other thriving Web entrepreneurs, avoids spending money on market research. He tests new products on himself and his friends, since they are like his target market.

Digg's stature changed dramatically that day. It is now the twenty-fourth most popular Web site in the United States, nipping at the *New York Times* (number 19) and easily beating Fox News (number 62), according to industry tracker Alexa.com. More than 1 million people flock to Digg daily, reading, submitting, or "digging" some 4,000 stories. As on many Web 2.0 sites, people register and create online profiles. Then these "diggers" can upload links to stories and blogs that they want to share from other news portals like Yahoo! News or mainstream media sites like the *Washington Post*. Users can click a "digg it" button that essentially casts a vote for the content. They can also hit the "bury" button. The stories with the most "diggs" zoom to the top of the page. Of the free labor that is the "Digg Army," 94 percent are male; more than half are IT types in their twenties and thirties making $75,000 or more. It's a demographic that advertisers lust after.

COMMUNITY FIRST, ADS LATER

That's why some smart money is on Digg to become an ad magnet like MySpace.com. Some even refer to Digg as the new *New York Times*. News sites are discovering that they can benefit, too: get a story on Digg's front page, and in comes a flood of traffic from people clicking on the link to read the story on your site. Digg gets advertising via Federated Media, the company that Silicon Valley veteran John Battelle created to pair Web sites with advertisers (Digg sparingly places ads in a narrow band at the top of the Web page). So far, Digg is breaking even on an estimated $3 million annually in revenues. Nonetheless, people in the know say that Digg is easily worth $200 million.

It's not as dot-com déjà vu as it sounds. YouTube, the enormously popular video site, posts similarly fledgling revenues, but some experts say that it could easily fetch $500 million. What's more, Digg registered users have been doubling every three months. As such, Digg is attempting to follow the path laid out by Google Inc. and now being adopted by many Web 2.0 companies: focus on building a user community, and the ads will follow. "It's one of those things where we know we could put crazy ads all over the site and clutter it up, but we don't want to do that," says Rose. "We have a clear path toward becoming a profitable company, and we're fully funded. We don't have to worry about it now, as long as we keep hitting our numbers."

It used to be that major companies, like Intel and Oracle, needed huge infusions of capital to get started. Today the barrier to entry is so low that Rose launched Digg with just a $99-a-month server, a $12-an-hour freelance coder, and $1,200 to buy the domain name.

So far, Digg has succeeded. But success has also brought copycats and stress. A rumored $40 million offer from Yahoo! Inc. surfaced in January, which Yahoo denied. Two weeks before the Digg.3 release, AOL launched a rival under the old Netscape brand. (It was headed up by former Silicon Alley superstar Jason M. Calacanis, owner of Weblogs, who early on had offered Rose an investment in Digg and an option to buy it for $5 million. That deal would have left Rose with no control. Forget it.) On July 18, AOL tried to lure Digg's top 50 contributors with $1,000 a month to switch to its site, which led Rose to rant on his weekly podcast that Calacanis and AOL were trying to "squash Digg." The corporate giant's failure to gain inroads so far shows that simply copying Digg won't work. It also spells out why Old Media types are so afraid of being eaten alive by the creative destruction that these young new players are delivering. The barriers to entry are now so low that all it takes is a laptop and a $50-a-month Internet hookup to make a kid the next mogul.

Rose hints that there's going to be more to Digg than just democratizing the news. In six months, he says, as he polishes off a Belgian beer at Fly Bar in San Francisco's Hayes Valley a week after the launch, the site will unveil new features that he can or.ly describe as "some really cool stuff." He's beaming as though he's talking about a new girl, and it's all he can do not to blurt out what all that cool stuff is. "Why would you sell unless you feel you've played your hand?" he asks.

The thought of selling all or even a large piece of his venture brings back some bad memories. Rose and all the other geeks know someone from the last boom who was worth millions one month, only to move into his parents' basement the next. Indeed, Valley-wide, guys like Rose, his entourage of buddies, and many others are haunted by the years when the weekly rooftop parties died, the traffic thinned, and no one needed restaurant reservations. This time around, the entrepreneurs worry that, within a moment, the money— and their projects—could vanish.

POWER MOVE

Web 2.0 entrepreneurs saw the dot-com flame-outs in the late 1990s and learned an important lesson: don't rely on paper riches. Unlike their predecessors, they are fiscally prudent. They don't burn through cash buying Aeron chairs or holding lavish parties.

ROCK STAR STATUS

But for now, Rose is the "It" boy among a new wave of entrepreneurs running the hottest of the top 100 Web 2.0 companies sprinkled around the Bay Area. Together, this network of mostly Valley boys—Six Apart Ltd. cofounder Mena Trott is a rare female among them—fill SF bars like Anu and Wish and Cav and parties at their sparsely furnished lofts.

Rose's social stock has climbed, too. He has more than 11,000 friends on MySpace. He was a runner-up in blog ValleyWag's "Hottest Guy in the Valley" contest (think Tom Cruise's doughier little brother), and he co-hosts a hot weekly video podcast called *Diggnation*. It's like a techie version of the *Saturday Night Live* skit "Wayne's World." He and Alex Albrecht, a former TechTV co-host, sit on a couch, drink beer, say "dude" a lot, and talk about the biggest stories that week. At a party for the fiftieth show, Rose was mobbed by fans and even photographed signing a pretty brunette's cleavage. The snapshot was posted on Flickr the next day, prompting one viewer to comment: "When did they become rock stars?"

Clearly much has changed since 1999, and Rose and his fellow wealth punks have little in common with the sharp-talking MBAs in crisp khakis and blue button-downs who rushed the Valley as the Nasdaq climbed. In the late 1990s, entrepreneurs were the supplicants, and Sand Hill Road, dotted with venture-capital firms, was the mecca. Dot-commers relied on VCs for the millions they needed to buy hardware, rent servers, hire designers, and advertise like crazy to bring in the eyeballs. For their big stakes of, say, $15 million for 20 percent of a company, venture capitalists received board seats, control of the management levers, and most of the equity.

> **POWER MOVE**
>
> Having seen dot-coms fall apart after venture capitalists took over, many founders of start-ups today will turn down lucrative investments so that they can stay in charge.

Now, it's more like: maybe we'll let you throw a few bucks our way—if you get it. Otherwise, get lost. That's possible because the cost of jump-starting a good idea has plummeted. At the same time, the sources of money have multiplied; it's swirling in from new VC shops, angel investors, and strategic partners galore. The awash-in-capital environment has flipped the power dynamic. Sure, they'll take money from the "sweater vests," as Digg CEO Jay Adelson calls the VCs, but they'll do it on their own terms. "It's a good time now for the entrepreneur," says John Freeman, a professor at University of California at Berkeley's Haas School of Business. "There are lots of different pots of money. It gives them the ability to modify when they take it, [and] how much they take, and leaves them with more control."

Who are some of the new geek elite? Besides Rose, there's his pal and Wall Street transplant Joshua Schachter, who recently sold Del.icio.us, a Web site to exchange favorite links, to Yahoo for an estimated $31 million; gaming whiz kid Dennis Fong, a.k.a. Thresh, cofounder of gaming company Xfire, which was sold to Viacom Inc. in April for $102 million; Mark Zuckerberg, who started the social networking site Facebook in college; and Jeremy Stoppelman and Russel Simmons, cofounders of Yelp.com, a consumer review site. The elder statesmen of the group are Hot or Not founder James Hong and his best friend, Max Levchin, who sold his company PayPal to eBay Inc. for $1.5 billion at 26 and is now engrossed in Slide.com, a start-up that delivers images to computers in a slick slide show format.

Digg is emblematic of the ethos of Web 2.0, new consumer and media sites revolving around social networking and do-it-yourself services. Others include YouTube, which serves up some 100 million requested videos a day, rivaling the audience of NBC. Then there's Facebook, where the college crowd practically lives. The average gamer on Xfire spends an astounding 91 hours a month on the site—it's like a part-time job. As a result, superhigh valuations are again coming out of the Valley. In a world in which Facebook turns down $600 million deals, the $580 million that Rupert Murdoch's News Corp. shelled out for MySpace.com in July 2005 is widely considered to be a steal.

> **POWER MOVE**
>
> Figuring out when, or if, to cash out is tricky. Josh Schachter sold his company, Del.icio.us, to Yahoo for an estimated $31 million, but some now believe that he sold too soon—missing out on the opportunity to become a reverse Google.

Those in the know believe that Digg could become a new kind of clearinghouse for news and that its interactive community concept could snowball. That could be a jackpot for Rose, who owns 30 to 40 percent of the company (he won't specify)— a massive stake for a founder in a world in which investors routinely demand up to 20 percent with every outlay. But it's still only paper wealth, which he and many others have learned can evaporate. "I was here in 2000," he recalls in an instant message.

It was just two years ago that Rose was the host of an obscure cable show, *The Screen Savers*, on a low-rent channel called TechTV. One day, he was at lunch with Apple Computer Inc. founder Steve Wozniak, a favorite interview subject. Woz was in a deep riff about the glamour of Apple's garage days, and Rose realized that he was jealous of Woz's place in Valley history. This guy has actually done things, Rose remembers thinking, while I'm, like, a visual stenographer. That night, Rose returned to his five-person Santa Monica house, head down, and plopped in front of his computer. Like every other night, he explored the back caves of the Internet, scavenging for hidden gossip and unearthed news that eluded most mainstream editors. They were all so clueless, Rose was thinking. And then it occurred to him: oh my God. I could do this SO MUCH BETTER.

BOTTOM-UP MEDIA

Soon, Rose was blabbing about his idea to his girlfriend, his buds, his bartenders. This would be bottom-up media. Citizen journalism. In the fall of 2004, Rose withdrew $1,000—nearly one-tenth of his life savings—and paid a freelance coder $12 an hour to mock up a Web page. He got a deal on server space over the Web for $99 a month. Only one big expense was left: the domain name. He tried Dig.com. *!@#! It was owned by Disney. He offered the owners of digdig.com $500. They wouldn't sell. Ouch. Finally he settled on Digg.com and forked out $1,200 to its owners. The site was launched on December 5, 2004.

Today, Rose is like one of those guys he used to interview. But he and his ilk have their detractors. Some say that Digg is just regurgitating news. Others accuse Web 2.0 entrepreneurs of trying to build businesses around little more than one cool feature. As always in the Valley, say critics, the froth floweth over.

Rose is listening to his gut, he says. Digg arose out of his everyday life, just as Facebook and YouTube and Xfire did for their founders. During the boom, MBAs dreamed up stuff that they thought could nab money. Today, the geeks insist that they're looking at ways in which technology can fill the gaps in their own lives. Then they build those services and share them with their friends. Once something works, they start to dribble it out to the world. But nothing too fancy that needs money to get started.

So the VCs aren't so mighty this time. There's intense competition among funders for pieces of Web 2.0. Two decades ago, nearly 300 VC firms invested in high tech. Last year, that number soared to 866 in the United States. Meanwhile, deal sizes for Internet companies are contracting, even as valuations for those deals almost doubled from 2004 to 2005 and are rising still. That means that investors are forced to take smaller stakes in Web deals, while entrepreneurs are holding on to more. Money is also coming from legends like Marc Andreessen of Netscape fame, who's backing Web 2.0 projects, as are rich friends Levchin and Hong. "Until capital becomes important again, venture capitalists are screwed," says Andrew Anker, a former VC at August Capital in Menlo Park, California, who decamped in 2003 for blogging start-up Six Apart.

Rose grew up in Las Vegas. His father is an accountant, and his mom "just chills," he says. They lived in a three-bedroom house on a cul-de-sac. Standard middle-class America. His love affair with computers drew scorn from other schoolkids, so Rose transferred to a public vo-tech in 1993 to study computers and animation. "It was a chance to be with other nerds," he says.

In 1999 he dropped out of the University of Las Vegas to join the action in Silicon Valley, where he took coding jobs for dot-coms. That led to his gig as the host of TechTV, which transferred him to Los Angeles in 2003. But Rose was bored. He hated L.A. If it hadn't been for his friendship with Adelson, he might never have pursued the Digg idea. The two met when Rose interviewed Adelson, 35, founder and chief technology officer of data center company Equinix, on TechTV in 2003. Here was another guy who was actually doing something. Rose and Adelson quickly hit it off. Adelson played the grown-up, a role he still relishes, saying things like, "Kevin, you're 29 now, you need to stop wearing your pants lower than your boxers" (advice that Rose still ignores). But he believed in Digg from the beginning.

POWER MOVE

One reason for Digg's success is that Rose hired a CEO who not only had the management skills but understood and shared his passion.

FORGET PORTALS

In February 2005, Rose cashed Digg's first investor check. It was for $50,000, and it came from a friend, Chris Hoar, who had founded Textamerica, a site that enables you to post cell phone photos to your blog. When Rose was desperate for servers, Hoar cut him a check on the spot. Digg didn't even have a company bank account yet, so Adelson walked Rose through the accounting and helped him drum up the next round, which was several hundred thousand dollars in investments from angel investors, including Andreessen and Reid Hoffman, CEO of social networking site LinkedIn.com Corp.

Rose asked Adelson to sign on as chief executive. Adelson had been burned during the last boom, when his net worth had dwindled from a high of $55 million, but he decided to take the job, even though it would mean commuting between New York, where his wife and three kids live, and San Francisco. There was something about Rose: he reminded Adelson of his younger, single self.

POWER MOVE

At a time when venture capitalists are clamoring to invest in new Web businesses, shrewd entrepreneurs can negotiate sweet deals. Facebook founder Mark Zuckerberg wangled $38 million and a clause that keeps him in charge as long as he wants.

By spring 2005, the venture set had caught on that something was happening at Digg. Adelson was fielding a call per week begging for a meeting, but he kept stalling. He wanted Digg to get more traction, to wait until it really needed the money. "I don't want to be someone's ticket into a market," Adelson says. When they started talking with VCs last August, Adelson recalls, a few asked about Digg's plans to convert its site into the next Yahoo or Google. "They are still back in the 1998 belief system that it's all about portals," Adelson says, laughing. "Grow up, man."

At an obscure office complex in San Mateo in August 2005, the reception was different. Greylock Partners is a storied VC firm with many home runs to its credit, but few dot-coms among them. Yet Greylock partner David Sze seemed to dig Digg. He himself was a member of the Digg Army. He understood Rose's of-the-people vision. "There were not a lot of in-between kind of guys," Rose says. "David got it, and most everyone else didn't."

Then Sze, 40, stunned them. Rose and Adelson were seeking only $1 or $2 million, pocket change to most Silicon Valley firms and hardly worth their time; VC firms usually make big bets to win big stakes. What firm has the resources to keep an eye on 100 companies? Funders had been trying to persuade them to take $5 million, or even $10 million, but Adelson stood firm. Sze agreed that they didn't need it and got his partnership to change the rules and green-light the small deal: $2.5 million, divided between Greylock and another firm, Omidyar Network, the venture fund of eBay founder Pierre Omidyar.

POWER MOVE

Internet audiences can be fickle, leading even successful early entrants to be replaced overnight. Friendster was hugely popular—until My Space came along and became the new phenomenon.

Digg was finally flush with enough cash to pay salaries, rent an office, and keep employees in standard start-up snacks like Twizzlers and Vitamin Water. Adelson did the hiring and managed the business, while Rose worked on Version 3.0. On trips home to Las Vegas or to see friends in L.A., Rose dreamed up at least one new feature per trip, like the Digg "stack," which visually shows users how stories are being ranked in real time, and a module for tracking friends' activity on the site.

But the consumer Web is still a crapshoot. As early social networking sites like Friendster learned the hard way, audiences can be fickle. "It's kind of like the entertainment business," says Berkeley's Freeman. "If it hits, it's big."

So far, Digg's traffic just keeps growing. And Rose is picking up a bit of swagger. His shyness is fading, and his wardrobe has gotten a hipster upgrade. Girls on MySpace swarm him. But the pain of losing his girlfriend isn't gone, and he says that no matter what happens with Digg, he won't put business first again.

The tech bust notwithstanding, the Valley is still the only place on earth where geeks with good ideas can become celebrities overnight. But wannabes be warned: as nearly everyone found out six years ago, the fall from rock star to pariah can be just as quick—and not nearly as much fun.

THE PROBLEM

Maintaining control of the start-up, while also bringing in investors who can provide financing and help the business grow

Finding and keeping consumers in a crowded market that continually attracts new competitors

THE SOLUTION

Recognize that the balance of power has shifted, giving entrepreneurs more room to bargain for what they want from financiers.

Keep users coming to your site by constantly developing fresh, new ideas that will serve their needs.

Increase the odds that a new product or service will be successful by testing it out on friends and others who are similar to your user base and refining it as necessary.

Keep overhead low, forgoing fancy offices and parties and outsourcing whatever you can.

Hire as CEO an experienced manager who understands and shares the founder's passion and vision, so that the founder can concentrate on creating the new products and ideas.

SUSTAINING THE WIN

Keep the focus on creating cool products that work well, rather than pouring money into marketing hype.

KEVIN ROSE

DAVID SCHOMER: HIGHER GROUNDS AT ESPRESSO VIVACE ROASTERIA

POWER PLAYER
David Schomer, the founder and owner of Espresso Vivace Roasteria, a $1.7 million coffee empire based in Seattle, is a pioneer in the high-quality coffee world. "I want every shot of espresso to taste as good as freshly ground coffee smells."

Stanley Holmes's profile of espresso impresario David Schomer appeared in the Winter 2007 edition of *BusinessWeek Small Business*.

OBSESSION WITH QUALITY

David Schomer had spent 16 years working toward this moment. It was February 2001, and Schomer, the owner of Espresso Vivace Roasteria in Seattle, was demonstrating an espresso machine that he had fitted with a device that solved one of the biggest problems in espresso making: water-temperature fluctuations that can make coffee taste burned or sour. A half-dozen industry veterans waited eagerly as Schomer pulled the first shots from the rejiggered machine. The espresso flowed smooth and thick as honey. "I had tears in my eyes," recalls the wiry, blunt-speaking 50-year-old. "I just could not believe it."

Conquering the temperature problem was the coup de grâce in Schomer's long struggle to create the perfect cup of espresso. The former Boeing engineer and musician had rethought every aspect of brewing espresso, from the freshness of the beans to the patterns that baristas make in the espresso's crema, the foam topping created during brewing. Along the way, Schomer documented his discoveries in trade journals and eventually a book and videos that were the first to promulgate standards for espresso making.

Schomer's manic devotion to quality and his willingness to share what he has learned have made him an icon in the clubby world of high-quality coffee. "What he did so well was the research in espresso making and creating the first training materials on standards and techniques for the industry," says Don Holly, director of quality at Green Mountain Coffee Roasters in Vermont and former administrative director for the Specialty Coffee Assn. Says Willem Boot, president of Boot Coffee Consulting & Training, who works with small U.S. roasters: "He is a true espresso professor."

Not surprisingly, Schomer's guru status has been very good for

POWER MOVE

Schomer approaches his business with the fervor and commitment of an artist. Dedicated to selling the very best espresso, he won't take shortcuts, and he works on improving every step of the process.

business. In a city awash in coffee, Vivace has gone from selling lattes and espresso from a street cart in 1988 to a 48-employee company that includes two Seattle coffeehouses. A retail arm sells coffee beans, as well as Schomer's book and videos, in its stores and online. Sales hit $1.7 million in 2006.

That may be a pittance in the $11 billion gourmet coffee industry. But Schomer is no Howard Schultz wannabe, and he harbors no desire to turn Vivace into the next Starbucks. Making coffee that meets his standards can't be done by a chain; it is far too labor-intensive and costly. "David's pursuit of perfection touches a customer base that's looking for that idealism and the expression of craftsmanship that Starbucks can never satisfy," says Holly. Instead, he aims for "manageable and sustained growth." As Schomer puts it: "I make coffee for people who love coffee. And I like that."

Schomer's espresso odyssey began after a few of his other passions fizzled. In 1987, weary of his long commute, Schomer quit his job as a measurements engineer at Boeing and studied classical flute at Cornish College of the Arts in Seattle. He awoke from his dream of becoming a professional musician as the bills mounted and he and his wife, Geneva Sullivan, had their first child. At the time, Seattle was becoming coffee-crazed, with coffeehouses cropping up everywhere and residents becoming connoisseurs of a type of rich, intense coffee that most of America had yet to taste. In 1988, Schomer and Sullivan, who now handles the company's accounting, used $12,000 in savings to start Vivace as an espresso cart on Broadway Avenue in the city's hip Capitol Hill neighborhood. At first, the Broadway Chamber of Commerce opposed the idea, but Schomer persuaded them by promising to provide classical musicians to play for his customers.

While many entrepreneurs are reluctant to divulge their "trade secrets," Schomer has found that sharing his knowledge in trade journals and instructional videos has turned him into an expert. That has paid off in all kinds of lucrative contracts, including sales of his coffee beans to other cafés.

MMM, CARAMEL

Four years later, Schomer borrowed $120,000 from a bank to open a 1,000-square-foot coffeehouse down the street from the cart. He began roasting beans in the back of the store in batches small enough to allow him to keep them fresh and capture the essential oils that create a sweet caramel taste and thick crema.

Vivace's coffee quickly won fans in Seattle and beyond. But Schomer was by no means satisfied. Frustrated by the inconsistent quality of his espresso shots, he tore apart the process, using an approach that he describes as "scientific precision guided by artistry." One by one, he tackled the problems. "Espresso took over my imagination," he says. Fresh beans, for example, are needed to create a rich crema, so Schomer began buying wholesale beans from brokers. He settled on a blend of high-quality arabica and robusta beans. "Robusta is not as elegantly flavored as arabica, but it produces a better crema," Schomer says. "It's a structural thing." He developed techniques for latte art in which baristas manipulate the cup and milk pitcher to create intricate ribbon patterns of leaves, hearts—even butterfly wings—in the foam atop lattes, cappuccinos, and macchiatos.

Schomer's biggest challenge was stabilizing an espresso machine's water temperature, which he discovered might vary from the ideal 203.5°F by as much as 8°. He modified machines by adding water tanks to hold the pressure steady, and then using a digital probe to determine when the water was at the optimal temperature. Then came his 2001 breakthrough: Schomer fitted a machine with a precision temperature control device adopted from the aerospace and manufacturing industries, limiting fluctuations to 2°. "It was the high point of my career," he says.

CREATIVE CULTURE

Schomer's reputation spread largely because he shared his knowledge. As soon as he mastered a step in the process, Schomer documented his technique in articles published in trade journals. In 1996, he collected his research in *Espresso Coffee: Professional Techniques*. He also produced two instructional videos, *Caffè Latte Art* and *Techniques of the Barista*. Although the book and videos account for only 4 percent of Vivace's revenues, they've been valuable tools for crafting and boosting his image.

As Schomer's standing in the industry rose, so did sales of his coffee beans to other cafés. Schomer now roasts about 3,000 pounds of beans a week to use in his shops and for retail sale, accounting for 25 percent of revenues. His high profile comes in handy when he negotiates a purchase price for the beans, as brokers often give him the best beans available, something that they rarely do for small companies. Schomer is now testing a coffee grinder he designed with an Italian company, La Marzocco, to be called the S Grinder. He will get a percentage of sales and 18 grinders to use in his stores. "My marketing clout is so much bigger from the writing and the videos," he says. "I have the credibility and the reach, and that's why La Marzocco is partnering with me."

To find baristas who share his passion, Schomer tries to create a culture that will appeal to independent people with a creative bent. "You have to have artistic individuals making the coffee," he says. "You have to capture their imagination and allow them to feel special, but you can't let them run over you." Training is extensive: newbies can pull shots only after six months of instruction, and even then they must be supervised by a veteran barista. "I can't have fools making this coffee," says Schomer. A full two years of training are necessary before a barista goes solo, an occasion that

POWER MOVE

High employee turnover is a problem for many small businesses. Schomer tries to improve employee retention by offering better-than-average salaries and generous benefit packages.

As most business owners know, it's not easy to find employees who share their dedication and skill. Schomer instituted an intensive training program to groom workers.

Schomer marks with a brief ceremony in which he gives the newly certified espresso maker a Vivace jacket. He holds monthly meetings with all employees to talk shop. "I loved that we would just talk about the quality, humidity issues, bad beans, maintenance of the machines," says Chad Smith, who was a Vivace employee for three years and is now a barista at another Seattle coffeehouse, Herkimer Coffee. Smith concedes that Schomer struggles with turnover because he is demanding, and many of his best people go on to start their own shops. "But it eventually trickles back to him because his competitors talk him up," says Smith. "You have people competing with him but who also tell their customers that he's the man."

Schomer woos employees with tangible benefits as well. Vivace pays baristas between $8 and $12 an hour, which is high for the industry. So payroll accounts for about 35 percent of operating costs, well above the industry average of 25 percent. Schomer tops it off with health benefits, a 401(k) plan, and paid vacation.

Last March, Schomer opened a second Seattle store, on Yale Avenue. The 2,000-square-foot space, financed with a $362,000 loan and $250,000 of personal funds, is an homage to espresso. A mural on the front of the bar counter illustrates the history of espresso and is painted with coffee pigments. Scattered across the rainforest-green and coffee-brown marble floor are mosaic tiles with renderings of latte art patterns. And Schomer has commissioned Kurt Wenner, an Italian painter, to create a mural entitled *Vivi Vivace i Vizu e le Virtu* ("Live intensely your vices and virtues"). It has worked well for Schomer.

THE PROBLEM

Creating a boutique business that will flourish despite strong competition

Finding ways to create and sell goods of extraordinarily high quality

THE SOLUTION

Investigate and experiment with new technologies and techniques to discover ways to improve the product.

Ensure that the customer experience is consistently superior by hiring carefully and putting all employees through in-depth training.

Use the founder's reputation as an industry expert to strike better deals with vendors and branch out into new ventures.

SUSTAINING THE WIN

Continue to strive for perfection by setting high standards and expectations, but also be supportive and encouraging so that employee morale and retention remain high.

DAVID SCHOMER

57

CHINA'S POWER BRANDS: MAINLAND ENTREPRENEURS VERSUS MULTINATIONALS

POWER PLAYERS
Bold entrepreneurs are producing Mainland China's hot consumer products. But the multinationals are fighting back. Who will the big winners be?

This 2004 International Edition cover story was reported by Dexter Roberts with Frederik Balfour, Bruce Einhorn, Michael Arndt, Michael Shari, and David Kiley.

LESSON PLAN

Embrace the trial-and-error process involved in expanding overseas. Expect to stumble and lose money on foreign ventures at first, as the company gains understanding and expertise in new markets.

Develop a keen appreciation for the different needs of consumers in different countries, and tailor products to meet those needs.

Grow the company by focusing on areas, that have not been claimed by the corporate behemoths.

Be willing to spend big bucks on advertising and research and development in order to create brand awareness.

BUILD A BRAND

How do you get rich in China these days? Build a brand. That's what 35-year-old Huang Guangyu has done. The Guangdong native started out at 18, renting a market stall in Beijing and hawking cheap plastic appliances. Today, his GOME Electrical Appliances is China's top consumer-electronics chain, with well over 100 stores, $2 billion in sales, and the kind of high-plateau brand recognition that Circuit City and Best Buy enjoy in the United States.

And thanks to a backdoor stock listing in Hong Kong this summer, Huang's net worth is at least $830 million. There's just one hitch, though. China's domestic retail players, including GOME, are already worried about the impact of foreign competition next year, when Beijing will open the entire country to retailers from abroad.

This little tale neatly sums up the story of China's emerging brands today: tremendous excitement about the brands, but a good dose of fear about their staying power. Global business executives are certainly agog at the prospect that the next stage of China's superfast development will be the establishment of power brands in everything from retailing to white goods to autos and more—brands that are strong enough to both dominate at home and thrive overseas. "They are definitely going global," says Glen Murphy, the Shanghai-based managing director of ACNielsen in China. "With their resources and production base, they are large enough to reach out to the world."

There are plenty of well-known local names besides GOME. Haier Group, of course, is the granddaddy, a $10 billion maker of refrigerators, washing machines, and more, with global ambitions nurtured by its well-known boss, Zhang Ruimin. Hangzhou Wahaha Group Co., with $1.2 billion in sales, is the top vendor of bottled water. TCL Corp., with $3.4 billion in revenue, is so powerful in TVs and other electronics that it reached a deal to merge its television business with that of France's Thomson last year and took control of Alcatel's cell phone business this year. Lenovo Group Ltd., formerly known as Legend, with

$3 billion in revenue, is number one in China's PC market. Li-Ning Co. Ltd., founded by a Chinese athlete, is the top seller of athletic footwear and apparel; it went public this year, too. The roster goes on and on.

But China brand watchers wonder, is this impressive enough? They see the capacity overhang in Chinese industry, the tendency to skimp on innovation, the ever-growing presence of multinationals on the mainland, and the continuing popularity of foreign brands on the mainland. Share prices for many of China's consumer brand companies are way off this year. Brand awareness of Chinese companies among U.S. and European consumers is, by and large, low. And for every China brands enthusiast, there's a skeptic. "Export their brands successfully?" asks Tom Doctoroff, CEO for Greater China at U.S. ad agency J. Walter Thompson. "Chinese companies are light-years away from it."

Then again, so were the Koreans when they set out 20 years ago to join the stable of world-class brand companies—and no one could have predicted that Samsung, LG, and Hyundai would be the up-and-coming global brands they are now. Like the Koreans, the Chinese are certainly going to stumble many times as they build their brands. But with all the furious activity going on in the marketplace, some of these brands will emerge as real winners, both at home and abroad. Unlike the nationalist Japanese, some will hook up with foreign companies to get a boost—and some will even use the brand name of their foreign partner when they market abroad, as TCL will with RCA, Thomson's big brand in the United States, and the Thomson brand itself, in Europe.

POWER MOVE

One way that companies can boost their chances of succeeding abroad is to strike deals with foreign companies that have the skills and name awareness that they lack. The $3 billion Chinese electronics giant TCL Corp., for instance, acquired Thomson-RCA's TV line and Alcatel's cell phone business, which gave it Western brand names, distribution networks in Europe, and Western technology.

China's huge domestic economy gives these contenders the chance to cut their teeth in the most competitive market on earth, and to build up a war chest of revenues for their efforts abroad. "Market shares will go up and down. Some Chinese companies will lose. It's a learning process," says Paul Gao, a principal in the Shanghai office of McKinsey & Co. "But there is no doubt that world-class Chinese brands will emerge." The learning process will involve both making better products and selling them more effectively. Ogilvy & Mather chairman and CEO Shelly Lazarus recently led a conference of more than a dozen Chinese companies at the former estate of agency founder David Ogilvy. Lazarus was impressed by both their lack of knowledge and their hunger. "Most Chinese companies don't yet understand even what we mean by 'positioning' a brand," Lazarus told *BusinessWeek*. "But they are anxious to know. They can't suck it in fast enough. They are going to figure this out. You can see it in their eyes."

THE COMPETITIVE CRUSH

Who will those winners be? China brand watchers pick TCL, Haier, and SVA, a top TV maker. But at this stage in China's tumultuous economy, it's hard to say for sure. Overcapacity has reached 30 percent in many industries, including televisions, washing machines, and refrigerators, putting tremendous pressure on margins. "Home electronics appliance prices are decreasing 10 to 15 percent annually," says Chen Kaixun, vice president of Hisense Electric Co. Ltd., an appliance maker and rival to Haier. "For the price war, the only thing we can do is decrease our costs." Hisense managed 2 percent profit growth in the first half. The price war has also hit Haier hard; its Shanghai-listed arm pulled off only 6 percent profit growth for the first

POWER MOVE

Companies that want to grow into global brands must invest heavily in research and development. The most successful multinationals typically spend 5 percent or more of revenues on R&D, recognizing that innovation and customer research are necessary if they are to stay ahead.

half, despite sharply rising sales. And it's not just white goods. Auto prices have fallen 7 percent in each of the past two years and are expected to drop at least 10 percent this year. The television glut is especially severe—and an aggressive export drive has triggered antidumping suits from the United States and Europe.

Another menace is the profusion of copycat products that spring up as soon as a brand gains popularity. Products from Tsingtao beer to Li-Ning shoes all compete with knockoffs. Often the only way for the big Chinese and foreign brands to drive the counterfeiters out of business is to slash prices even further—a strategy that runs counter to developing brand equity.

In this punishing environment, the until-now mediocre record of Chinese companies in innovation is a liability. It's rare for Chinese companies to meet the international norm of spending 5 percent or more of revenues on research and development. This spending gap can give multinationals the edge.

That's what has happened in cell phones. Between 2000 and 2003, local handset brands like Bird, Amoi, Panda, and TCL beat Nokia, Motorola, and other global brands on price and flashy features like TCL's gem-studded phone, a big success with the nouveaux riches. The locals went from a zero share in handsets a few years ago to almost 50 percent. "We take our Chinese competitors seriously," says Maurice Tan, marketing manager for Nokia China. "They are like a wolf pack."

Yet the wolf pack has been retreating of late. In the past year or so, Motorola, Nokia, and Sony Ericsson have rolled out a raft of phones with fancy new functions, pushed aggressively into new markets, and slashed prices. Nokia, for example, has added Chinese handwriting functions and expanded its relationships

POWER MOVE

Smaller businesses can achieve growth by selling primarily in the less-developed regions and markets that the giants ignore. In creating low-budget refrigerators and air conditioners in rural areas, Guangdong Kelon Electrical Holdings Co. created a successful niche for itself.

POWER MOVE

Designing and producing goods in the same country that you're selling in can give you a competitive advantage. When Haier Group, the Chinese appliance maker, designed its products in China and tried to sell them to the United States, the firm discovered that the products didn't quite meet American consumers' needs. So now it has 22 overseas factories and uses a "three-in-one strategy" of putting design, production, and sales in one country.

with the thousands of small retailers that sell mobile phones across China. Because of the counterattack, TCL has seen its share of the branded handset market slip from 8 percent to 6.1 percent in the last year and a half: Sales of its mobile phones at its Shenzhen-listed arm dropped almost by a third in the first half, while Bird's sales dropped almost 20 percent. Overall, domestic vendors have seen their handset sales slip from 42 percent of the market last year to 37 percent in the first half of 2004. Says Patrick Kung, general manager of Motorola's handset business in North Asia: "The locals did very well in the past three years. But starting this year, their growth rate has stalled big time." And there are still 37 local handset makers slugging it out.

Foreign manufacturers such as Hitachi and Samsung have also won back share in high-end plasma and flat-screen TVs, while Panasonic and LG have recovered some of the sales they lost in microwaves to local brand Galanz. In autos, the Koreans and Japanese are expected to introduce more affordable models in China. "The next several years will be difficult for local carmakers," predicts Yale Zhang, director of emerging-markets vehicle forecasts at CSM Asia Corp. in Shanghai. General Motors, Ford, and Volkswagen already offer budget models for less than $10,000. That could spell trouble for Geely Auto, a six-year-old brand that has quickly captured 4 percent of the market with cars that sell for as little as $3,500. Geely can't match the foreign brands for quality.

The increasing competition in retail will also hurt, at least in the short run. Today, Chinese companies have an edge in developing relationships with the thousands of small stores and kiosks where most Chinese shop. But with the World Trade Organization–mandated opening of all China to foreign retailers coming at the end of the year, multinationals such as Wal-Mart Stores Inc. and Carrefour will further expand their franchises, making those ties less important. "As the distribution model changes, it is becoming less and less suited to domestic brands, making it easier for foreign companies to penetrate China," says Qu Honglin, general manager of Local Strategy, a Shanghai brands consultancy.

A final issue that Chinese companies have to struggle with is the depth of management. Many of China's best brands were conceived by heroic entrepreneurs like GOME's Huang or 59-year-old Zong Qinghou. Zong, who spent years laboring in the rice paddies during the Cultural Revolution, is the founder of Wahaha, a beverage group that had profits of $196 million last year. (French company Groupe Danone owns 30 percent.) A hands-on leader, Zong will lead his managers on a tour of street vendors to see how beverages get sold in China's sprawling sidewalk markets. But he scorns market research, and it's not clear how Wahaha would fare without its charismatic founder. That's also true of other Chinese companies, says Local Strategy's Qu.

DON'T SKIMP ON R&D

These are all formidable problems. Yet for every setback, the Chinese find a way to move forward. Indeed, losing a few rounds in the most competitive market on earth is excellent training. Look at Lenovo. Several years ago, the computer maker hatched big plans to branch out into PDAs, mobile phones, and other areas beyond its expertise in laptops, PCs, and servers. The company pushed its global expansion as well. Bad idea. The loss of focus started costing Lenovo—as Dell Inc. stepped up the pressure in China. Lenovo had to lay off 5 percent of its workforce last

POWER MOVE

The new onslaught of foreign competition on Chinese soil is teaching Chinese start-ups a valuable lesson. To succeed in the long run, they must have layers of skilled management, not just a charismatic leader at the top.

spring. But to its credit, the company has refocused its priorities in the China market, and profits rebounded 24 percent in the first quarter of its fiscal year. Investors need to keep a watch, though. Lenovo is now going into investment banking—not exactly a core competence.

Other companies are realizing that they can't skimp on research. Over the next few years, TCL will ramp up R&D from 3 percent of sales to 5 percent. Television maker SVA Group spends 6 percent. "We must invest and develop new products," says Chen Hong, SVA's vice president in charge of overseas markets. "If we focus on price alone, we don't have a future." SVA sells only flat-screen and plasma televisions in the United States and has hired McKinsey to do consumer research to tailor its branded products.

If foreign connections will help, so be it. SVA has a new joint venture with NEC to manufacture LCD panels. TCL, by acquiring Thomson-RCA's TV line and Alcatel's cell phone business, has acquired Western brand names, distribution networks in Europe, and a bundle of Western technology. Strong sales in televisions in China and abroad helped push up TCL'S first-half earnings by 44 percent, despite its serious setback in cell phones at home.

One brand that has seen its global future and acted on it is telecom equipment maker Huawei Technologies Co. It already spends more than 10 percent of its revenues on research—and not only is competing successfully against outfits like Cisco in telecommunications gear but could emerge as a consumer brand as well. It now makes handsets and set-top boxes for TVs. Its formidable research machine could give it a winning hand.

POWER MOVE

Diversifying into new areas while also undertaking a costly global expansion is financially risky. Computer maker Lenovo had to lay off 5 percent of its workforce after it started selling PDAs and mobile phones.

Other companies are building up their knowledge of foreign markets. Haier has been criticized for not grasping what it takes to succeed globally. "One of the steps that many of the Asian companies have missed is the huge investment that's required to build brand equity," says David L. Swift, executive vice president of Whirlpool Corp.'s North American region, which competes with Haier. In the United States, Haier's greatest success is with budget items such as compact refrigerators.

Yet Haier already spends 4 percent of revenues on research and is creating local product-development teams in Tokyo and the United States to differentiate its line and move upmarket. In Japan, for instance, Haier offers washers that use less water, are quieter, and are narrow enough to fit into cramped Japanese homes. "In the past, we tried to design our products in Qingdao and sell them to the United States and Japan," says 55-year-old CEO Zhang. "They didn't meet overseas consumers' needs and didn't sell well." Today, Haier has 22 factories overseas, including a refrigerator plant in Camden, South Carolina. Revenues from Haier's overseas operations are up 53 percent to $1.3 billion in the first eight months of 2004.

Back home, many parts of the Chinese market are still up for grabs, thanks to the vastness of the country. Wahaha, for example, has built up its market by avoiding head-on confrontations with PepsiCo Inc. and Coca-Cola Co. and focusing on less-developed markets. It is now a big force in provincial capitals like Kunming, Yunnan. "We have a huge advantage in second-tier markets," boasts Wahaha's Zong, whose brand leads Coke and Pepsi in most of rural China. "In rural China, Wahaha has a majority position," confirms Zhu Huican, an analyst at Beijing market researcher Gung Ho Group.

Other companies are customizing products for the hinterland. Guangdong Kelon Electrical Holdings Co. has developed the budget Combine brand of refrigerators and air conditioners for less affluent consumers. "We are targeting poor families and farmers," says Kelon chairman Gu Chujun, a 45-year-old former scientist who patented his own

POWER MOVE

Companies that want to enter overseas markets should be prepared to lose money initially. Creating a global procurement, design, and production network will take time and money, but if it is done properly, it can pay off in the long term.

cooling system for his fridges. Kelon's sales are up 49 percent this year, while profits are up 11 percent.

Chinese companies are also learning how to raid the competition. Li-Ning has hired Wu Xianyong, a former Procter & Gamble manager, to run its marketing and branding. Wu made sure that many of the Chinese athletes at the Athens Olympics wore Li-Ning shoes and other equipment. Such product placement gave Li-Ning an Olympic boost in sales in China, where the company has more than 2,000 outlets and the top spot in athletic shoes, with 12.39 percent market share, according to Sinomonitor International, a Beijing market-monitoring firm.

POWER MOVE

Fostering brand awareness in a foreign market may require spending heavily on promotion. Since SVA, China's high-end TV maker, is not well known in the United States, the company spends 1 percent of revenues on advertising and marketing in the United States.

"All of us [Chinese consumer goods] companies must thank P&G for our development," says Li-Ning's general manager Zhang Zhiyong. Geely's Nan Yang, a senior vice president for overseas production, was formerly general manager of Shanghai Volkswagen Automotive Co., the joint venture between Volkswagen and Shanghai Automotive Industry Corp. Nan has overseen Geely's push into parts of the Arab world. The head of Wahaha's Future Cola unit once was the Beijing bottler for Pepsi.

Like Westerners, the Chinese are learning how to advertise on a grand scale. Ad spending last year was $24 billion in China, making it the third-biggest ad market in the world. A big chunk of that spending was by Chinese companies, and lines such as Li-Ning's "Anything is possible" are known by millions. The ad spending will only increase as the 2008 date of the Beijing Olympics approaches. Lenovo has already become the first Chinese company ever to be an official "top" sponsor of an Olympics—up there with Coca-Cola and Panasonic— when it signed on to back the 2008 games. It's part of "a longtime dream to become an international brand," says marketing boss Alice Li.

Sports marketing is a fast-rising category even without the coming Olympics. To keep its brand front-of-mind in China, SVA bought Shanghai's soccer team in 2001. Meanwhile, the world beckons. SVA has established its foothold in the United States. Meanwhile, TCL, with the Alcatel deal it just signed, has big plans for Europe. Geely has borrowed from the Koreans' early marketing strategy and entered other developing countries as a first step to overseas expansion, starting with the Middle East. On October 10, Haier announced that it is opening an R&D center and factory in fast-growing India.

Some of these efforts will fail. But with every ad campaign, every marketing battle, every product launch, the Chinese learn more. Does another Chinese juggernaut like the one that has taken over much of global manufacturing lie ahead? Not now. But give them time, and the best of these brands will prove themselves.

THE PROBLEM

Maintaining dominance in the domestic market when faced with new competition from multinationals

Successfully exporting products to other countries, where rival, homegrown brands are far better known and established

THE SOLUTION

Make innovation a high priority, allocating 5 percent of revenues to research and development, as most blue chips do.

Remain a leader at home by ensuring that the business is well run. Hire and train capable managers, rather than relying on the strengths of the founder/entrepreneur.

Partner with a foreign company that has strong name recognition and understands the local market.

Establish factories in each country where the company wants to sell, so that the products are designed and manufactured to meet the specific needs of the consumers there.

Work diligently and aggressively to forge positive relationships with local retailers. Don't assume that they'll take your product just because it's well made.

SUSTAINING THE WIN

Reserve the necessary resources for global expansion efforts by being cautious and conservative about launching other new and expensive ventures at the same time.

JEFF BEZOS:
AMAZON'S RISKY BET

POWER PLAYER

Chief executive, Jeff Bezos' big spending early on to expand Amazon from an online bookshop to a Web department store backed by a massive distribution system led some analysts to predict its demise. Not only has Bezos' company—once derided as "Amazon.toast" and "Amazon.bomb" —survived, it has thrived!

This 2006 cover story by Robert Hof looks at Jeff Bezos' next big step.

Make long-term bets, investing in initiatives that have lots of promise but may take years to yield big payoffs.

Champion creative, new ideas, even if they contradict conventional wisdom.

Put the focus on the customer, devising programs, strategies, and ideas that will help make the consumer experience more satisfying.

Embrace failure, understanding that some new ventures may not work, but that those that do will help the company thrive and endure.

MINDING THE STORE

It was one of the Web's typical flash frenzies, a gaggle of geeks seeking the newest new thing. At 2 a.m. on August 24, a new venture called Elastic Compute Cloud was quietly launched in test mode. Its service: cheap, raw computing power that could be tapped on demand over the Internet just like electricity. In less than five hours, hundreds of programmers, hoping to use the service to power their MySpace and Google wannabes, had snapped up all the test slots. One desperate latecomer instant-messaged a $10,000 offer for a slot to a lucky winner, who declined to give it up. "It's really cool," enthuses entrepreneur Luke Matkins, who will run his soon-to-launch music site on the service. The creator of this très cool service: Amazon.com Inc.

Yes, Amazon founder and Chief Executive Jeffrey P. Bezos, the onetime Internet poster boy who quickly became a post-dot-com piñata, is back with yet another new idea. Many people continue to wonder if the world's largest online store will ever fulfill its original promise to revolutionize retailing. But now Bezos is plotting another new direction for his 12-year-old company, which he will lay out on November 8 at San Francisco's Web 2.0 Conference, the annual gathering of the digerati crème. Judging from an advance look that he gave *BusinessWeek* on one recent gray day at Amazon's Seattle headquarters, it's so far from Amazon's retail core that you may well wonder if he has finally slipped off the deep end.

Bezos wants Amazon to run your business, at least the messy technical and logistical parts of it, using the same technologies and operations that power his $10 billion online store. In the process, Bezos aims to transform Amazon into a kind of twenty-first-century digital utility. It's as if Wal-Mart Stores Inc. had decided to turn itself inside out, offering its industry-leading supply chain and logistics systems to any and all outsiders, even rival retailers. Except Amazon is starting to rent out just about everything it uses to run its own business, from rack space in its 10 million square feet of warehouses worldwide to spare computing capacity on its thousands of servers, data storage on its disk drives, and even some of the millions of lines of software code it has written to coordinate all that.

Another big idea from Jeff Bezos? Go ahead and groan. It's fine with him. Even after all these years spent battling claims that his company would be "Amazon.toast," he's still bounding up and down stairs two at a time to exhort his band of nerds on to the Next Big Thing. And now, more than ever, he's determined to keep going for the big score, even if people think he's crazy. In fact, Bezos, 42, sounds downright eager to confound a new generation of skeptics. "We're very comfortable being misunderstood," he says, letting loose one of his famously thunderous laughs. "We've had lots of practice."

But if techies are wowed by Bezos' grand plan, it's not likely to win many converts on Wall Street. To many observers, it conjures up the ghost of Amazon past. During the dot-com boom, Bezos spent hundreds of millions of dollars to build distribution centers and computer systems in the promise that they eventually would pay off with outsize returns. That helped set the stage for the world's biggest Web retail operation, with expected sales of $10.5 billion this year.

What it didn't translate into was the consistent profit growth that many investors had expected until the past couple of quarters. A decline in Amazon's rate of spending-drowth, as well as a rise in sale growth thanks to the benefit of new retail initiatives, boosted profits and sent Amazon's stock price soaring. But the new digital utility services haven't yet take off. "I have yet to see how these investments are producing any profit," gripes Piper Jaffray & Co. analyst Safa Rashtchy. "They're probably more of a distraction than anything else."

What's more, at the same time Bezos is thinking big thoughts, Amazon's retail business is facing new threats. Its 25 percent sales growth tracks a little above the pace of overall e-commerce

POWER MOVE

Decisions can be easier if you take the time to study and do the math. Amazon wasn't sure that its TV ads were paying off, so it ran a 16-month test in two cities. The result: Bezos nixed the ads and spent the money on free e-shipping offers instead.

One of Jeff Bezos' strengths is that he has always championed bold, new ideas, even when they go against the conventional wisdom. Publishers said that Bezos was nuts to let customers post negative product reviews on his site. The reviews, which presaged the social Web phenomenon, have become one of Amazon's most popular features.

expansion and is nearly double its own pace way back in 2001. But other sites are fast becoming preferred first stops on the Web. Google, for one, has replaced retail sites such as Amazon as the place where many people start their shopping. And more personalized and social upstarts such as News Corp.'s MySpace and YouTube, which Google is buying, have become the prime places for many people to gather online—and eventually shop. It's a trend that Amazon could have trouble catching up to. Says consultant Andreas Weigend, Amazon's chief scientist until 2004: "The world has shifted from e-business to me-business."

With all those problems, some might view Bezos' latest tech toys as an attempt to take people's eye off the ball. But spend some time with Bezos, and it becomes clear that there may well be a method to his madness. Amazon has spent 12 years and $2 billion perfecting many of the pieces behind its online store. By most accounts, those operations are now among the biggest and most reliable in the world. "All the kinds of things you need to build great Web-scale applications are already in the guts of Amazon," says Bezos. "The only difference is, we're now exposing the guts, making [them] available to others."

And, he hopes, making money. With its Simple Storage Service, or S3, Amazon charges businesses 15 cents per gigabyte per month to store data and programs on Amazon's vast array of disk drives. It's also charging other merchants about 45 cents per square foot per month for real space in its warehouses. Through its Elastic Compute Cloud service, or EC2, it's renting out computing power, starting at 10 cents an hour for the equivalent of a basic server computer. And it has set up a semiautomated global marketplace for online piecework, such as transcribing snippets of podcasts, called Amazon Mechanical Turk. Amazon takes a 10 percent commission on those jobs.

Bezos is initially aiming these services at start-ups and other small companies with a little tech savvy. But it's clear that businesses of all kinds are the ultimate target market. Amazon has already attracted some high-powered customers. Microsoft Corp. is using the storage service to help speed software downloads, for instance, and the service is helping Linden Lab handle the crush of software downloads for its fast-growing Second Life online virtual world. Highly anticipated search upstart Powerset Inc. plans to use the Amazon computing service, even though it's still in test mode, to supplement its own computers when it launches its service sometime next year. And the search engine marketing firm Efficient Frontier uses Mechanical Turk to determine the most effective keywords for driving traffic to Web sites.

By all accounts, Amazon's new businesses bring in a minuscule amount of revenue. Although the direct cost of providing them appears relatively low because the hardware and software are in place, Stifel Nicolaus & Co. analyst Scott W. Devitt notes: "There's not going to be any economic return from any of these projects for the foreseeable future." Bezos himself admits as much. But with several years of heavy spending already, he's making this a priority for the long haul. "We think it's going to be a very meaningful business for us one day," he says. "What we've historically seen is that the seeds we plant can take anywhere from three, five, seven years to develop."

> **POWER MOVE**
>
> Amazon has become the Macy's of the Web by remaining, above all, customer-centric. Whether it's keeping prices low or pouring money into back-end operations, Amazon has devoted money, time, and energy to satisfying customers so that they keep coming back and spending even more.

A DARK HORSE IN A HIGH-STAKES RACE

Those initiatives may provide a boost for Amazon's retail side sooner than that. For one thing, they potentially make a profit

Like so many chief executives, Bezos recognizes that he has to evangelize for risky new ventures to win public buy-in. So when Amazon undertook a new effort to sell its data, computing power, and storage to other businesses, Bezos made the company's case to the media, explaining why this unorthodox strategy would be a good thing.

center out of the idle computing capacity needed for that retail operation. Like most computer networks, Amazon's uses as little as 10 percent of its capacity at any one time just to leave room for occasional spikes. It's the same story in the company's distribution centers. Keeping them humming at higher capacity means that they operate more efficiently, besides giving customers a much broader selection of products. And the more stuff Amazon ships, whether its own inventory or others', the better the deals it can cut with shippers.

But there's much more at stake for Bezos than making a few extra bucks selling services that his online store is already providing for itself. This is nothing less than a bid to lead the next wave of the Internet. A dozen years in the making, the economy that has grown up with the Internet by most accounts remains in its infancy. And leadership of that burgeoning economy remains up for grabs.

Google and Microsoft, in particular, are each angling to be the Net's kingpins. Just as Microsoft ruled the PC world (and its profits) with Windows software, so Google and Microsoft want to build what techies call the "platform" for the Web—the powerful layer of basic services on top of which everyone else builds their Web sites. "Amazon's a pretty serious dark horse" in that race, says Internet visionary Tim O'Reilly, CEO of tech publisher O'Reilly Media Inc. "Jeff really understands that if he doesn't become a platform player, he's at the mercy of those who do."

Bezos believes that he has identified a unique Amazonian edge: like no other Internet or computer company today, the e-retailer is in a position to apply the efficiencies of the Net to tangible and corporeal assets like products and people. Bezos envisions embedding the tasks of product distribution and knowledge work right into the flow of more automated business processes such as order taking and payment processing. For instance, a new service called Fulfillment by Amazon lets small and midsize businesses send their inventory to Amazon warehouses. Then when a customer places an order, Amazon gets an automated signal to ship it out—no muss, no fuss, no servers or software or garages full of stuff. "Amazon's in the business of managing complexity," says Amazon director John Doerr of the venture firm Kleiner Perkins Caufield & Byers. "There's no other e-commerce player that does that."

POWER MOVE

Taking a long view is critical if you want to build a brand that will thrive and endure, outlasting all competitors. Bezos is proud of hanging tough and making "seven-year bets," investing in projects that take years to become profitable.

Mundane as these business-focused services may sound, the implications for the economy at large are startling. Google, MySpace, and YouTube cracked open for the masses the means to produce media and the advertising that sustains it, creating tens of billions of dollars in market value and billions more in new revenues. Now, by sharing Amazon's infrastructure on the cheap, Bezos is taking that same idea into the realm of physical goods and human talent, potentially empowering a whole new swath of businesses beyond the Internet itself.

The upshot: while Wall Street yawns, Bezos' pioneering dot-com is actually starting to look almost hip again, at least to the all-important Web 2.0 geek gods who set the Net agenda today. More importantly, some venture capitalists have noticed, and they're encouraging their start-ups to consider using Amazon services to save money and get to market faster. "Amazon is becoming a very interesting company," says Crosslink Capital general partner Peter Rip. "They're taking their store in the sky and unbundling it."

In any case, this looks like Bezos' biggest bet since he and his wife, MacKenzie, drove west in 1994 to seek fame and fortune on the Net. Since then, he has survived the dot-com boom and bust with his ambitions intact. Now with three sons, and a daughter recently adopted from China, Bezos still has managed to find time to start a rocket company, Blue Origin. The venture is building a test facility in West Texas not far from his grandfather's ranch, where he once spent summers branding cattle. A longtime space nut, he made a valedictorian speech in 1982 at Miami Palmetto Senior High School about the need to colonize space.

Amazon, however, commands his full attention, especially now that the groundwork has been laid for the company's latest transformation. He began not long after the dot-com bust in 2001 with—big surprise—a huge project to modernize Amazon's massive collection of data centers and the software running on them. The result was that Amazon made it much faster and easier to add new Web site features. Small, fast-moving groups of five to eight Amazon employees now could go hog wild with new ideas, such as customer discussion boards on each product page and software to play music and videos on the site. Since then, these "two-pizza teams," as Bezos calls them because each team can be fed with two large pies, have become Amazon's prime innovation engines. "There's a huge value in this small, nimble team approach," says tech consultant and author John Hagel III. "But you can't do that without this kind of computer architecture."

POWER MOVE

Despite growing ever larger, Amazon has remained a nimble innovator by keeping product development teams small. With only five to eight people working together on each new idea, groups are able to brainstorm and mobilize quickly.

Next came an epiphany: if the new computer setup allowed folks inside to be more creative and independent, why not open it up to outsiders, too? So in 2002, Amazon began offering outside software and Web site developers access to selected Amazon data such as pricing trends, gradually adding more and more until this year. Now it's basically getting free help from more than 200,000 outside Web developers, up 60 percent from a year ago. They're building new services on top of Amazon technology, further feeding back into Amazon's core retail business. One service, Scanbuy, lets people check Amazon prices on their cell phones to see if they're better than prices in a retail store.

NEW SPARK PLUGS FOR START-UPS

Since its debut, the service has attracted thousands of "Turkers" working for dozens of companies. They're doing jobs that Mechanical Turk director Peter Cohen says "couldn't be done at all before," because there was no economical way to gather people for these tiny, often ephemeral tasks. Efficient Frontier has used the service to analyze tens of thousands of search keywords to see which of them best attract potential shoppers to particular Web sites. "There have not been any other services like Mechanical Turk that can do this so efficiently," says software engineer Zachary Mason.

Forget for a moment whether this will eventually turn us all into low-paid pieceworkers. The important thing is that the service is nurturing start-ups. CastingWords cofounder Nathan McFarland uses Turkers—who he says are largely the "bored and nothing-on-TV" set who treat the tasks like crossword puzzles— not only to transcribe 10-minute podcast segments, but also to assemble them into full transcriptions and to check the quality. Eighteen-year-old Eric Cranston, a onetime Turker living with his parents in Visalia, California, plans to use the service for a company he's starting that will retouch photos for Web sites. Essentially, Bezos sees the thousands of people from all over the world working inside Mechanical Turk's online marketplace as a big "human computer."

Amazon's other new services are getting even more serious attention. Last March, Amazon introduced its Simple Storage Service, which offers cheap space on its disk drives that any programmer or business can use to store data. Right away, Amazon approached an online photo-sharing start-up called SmugMug Inc. It was an ironic choice: president and cofounder Chris MacAskill had fiercely battled Amazon in an earlier start-up, an online bookstore called Fatbrain, which was later bought by Barnes and Noble.com. But MacAskill's son Don, SmugMug's cofounder and CEO, says that when he heard how easily and

If a company wants to innovate, it has to be willing to take risks and make some mistakes. Amazon has had its clunkers, like its failed search site, A9.com, but as Bezos says, "We're willing to go down a bunch of dark passageways . . . occasionally we find something that really works."

cheaply SmugMug could back up its photos on S3, "my eyes got all big." Now, by zapping customers' photos to Amazon to store on its servers, he's avoiding the need to buy more storage devices of his own—and saving $500,000 a year. "Everything we can get Amazon to do, we will get Amazon to do," says Chris MacAskill. "You're going to see all kinds of start-ups get a much better and faster start" by using Amazon's services.

They already are. Consider Powerset, the secretive search start-up backed by A-list angel investors, including PayPal Inc. cofounder Peter Thiel and veteran tech analyst Esther Dyson. Cofounder and CEO Barney Pell harbors ambitions of out-Googling Google with technology that he says would let people use more natural language than terse keywords to do their searches. By analyzing the underlying meaning of search queries and documents on the Web, Powerset aims to produce much more relevant results than the current search king's.

The problem is, Powerset's technology eats computing power like a child munches Halloween candy. The little 22-person company would have to spend more than $1 million on computer hardware, two-thirds of that just to handle occasional spikes in visitor traffic, plus a bunch of people to staff a massive data center and write software to run it. That's when Pell heard about Elastic Compute Cloud. He was sold. Based on tests so far, using the Amazon site for part of the company's computing power could cut its first-year capital costs alone by more than half.

Not least, Amazon is now opening its vast network of more than 20 distribution centers worldwide to all comers. For years it has handled distribution and even Web site operations for the likes of Target Stores Corp. and Borders Group. Recently it has started providing customized handling, packing, and customer service people for upscale retailers and manufacturers such as fashion boutique Bebe. And with Fulfillment By Amazon, it's opening all that up to small and midsize businesses.

With all these initiatives, Amazon empowers new start-ups that are hungry to knock off Internet leaders that happen to be . . . Amazon's competitors. Has Bezos thought about how he may be creating an army of allies to fight his rivals? His answer: "Absolutely!"

It's hard to dismiss another possibility, though: Amazon is biting off more than it can chew. Some of the new tech projects have come out with a thud. Compared with Google's, Amazon's A9.com search site never got traction, and its features were recently downsized. The new Amazon Unbox Video downloading service struck many early reviewers as clunky and slow.

Mostly, it's unclear whether Bezos can escape his and Amazon's linoleum-floor image. Amazon's mission to be the place where "customers can find and discover anything they might want to buy online" doesn't especially mesh with the goal of being the prime source of the services needed to run an Internet Age business. By contrast, nearly all of Google's services are clearly aimed at building the dominant digital utility. Likewise, IBM is much better known as a provider not only of technology services but also of expertise in automating a wider range of business processes, from inventory management to sales tracking.

POWER MOVE

While many people believe that companies need to squash their competitors, Amazon has invited outsiders in when they can provide more revenue. For instance, Amazon says that about 30 percent of its unit sales come from outside merchants' products listed and sold on its site.

Can Bezos manage a company that simultaneously sells the most routine stuff to consumers and the most demanding business services to entrepreneurs and corporations?

So Jeff Bezos faces a managerial moment of truth. Having saved Amazon from oblivion years ago, he nonetheless must prove that his latest big bet can help transform the company into something truly enduring. Not only does he make no apologies for such wagers, he revels in them. Every year in his annual letter to shareholders, he resurrects his 1997 letter, which reads in part: "We will make bold rather than timid investment decisions where we see a sufficient probability of gaining market leadership advantages."

Today, it's just the same. "We are willing to go down a bunch of dark passageways," he says, "and occasionally we find something that really works." As always, investing in Bezos and his company will require faith that there's light at the end of his newest tunnel—not just a money pit.

THE PROBLEM

Continuing to offer cutting-edge products and services so that the company remains a market leader

Creating new revenue streams by aggressively expanding into new, uncharted territory while withstanding criticism and doubt from others

THE SOLUTION

Make sure there are no sacred cows. Carefully study the age-old strategies to evaluate their cost-effectiveness, and ditch those that no longer work.

Invest heavily in creating superior "back-end" operations so that the organization can serve large numbers of customers.

Reject the old thinking of competitors as enemies, and be willing to sell those competitors products and services that will increase the company's profits and long-term viability.

Win over skeptics by becoming a company evangelist, explaining the company's vision with passion and logic.

SUSTAINING THE WIN

Stay committed to providing the same level of excellence in the organization's core areas, while identifying and expanding into new markets.

JEFF BEZOS

LINUS TORVALDS: LINUX INC.

POWER PLAYER

Linus Torvalds once led a ragtag band of software geeks. Not anymore. Here's an inside look at how the unusual Linux business model is increasingly threatening Microsoft.

This 2005 cover story by Steve Hamm profiles the Finnish tech guru Linus Torvalds.

LESSON PLAN

Reach a wide market by creating a versatile product, one that has the ability to serve clients of different sizes with different needs.

Cultivate a meritocratic environment by inviting everyone to contribute so that the most talented workers gain influence and responsibility.

Don't just preach fairness. Walk the talk, showing a zero tolerance for nepotism.

Learn to delegate and cede control, so that the company can move more quickly and people feel empowered to get their work done.

A NEW MODEL

Five years ago, Linus Torvalds faced a mutiny. The reclusive Finn had taken the lead in creating the Linux computer operating system, with help from thousands of volunteer programmers, and the open-source software had become wildly popular for running Web sites during the dot-com boom. But just as Linux was taking off, some programmers rebelled. Torvalds's insistence on manually reviewing everything that went into the software was creating a logjam, they warned. Unless he changed his ways, they might concoct a rival software package—a threat that could have crippled Linux. "Everybody knew things were falling apart," recalls Larry McVoy, a programmer who played peacemaker. "Something had to be done."

The crisis came to a head during a tense meeting at McVoy's house, on San Francisco's Twin Peaks. A handful of Linux's top contributors took turns urging Torvalds to change. After an awkward dinner of quiche and croissants, they sat on the living room floor and hashed things out. Four hours later, Torvalds relented. He agreed to delegate more and to use a software program for automating the handling of code. When the program was ready in 2002, Torvalds was able to process contributions five times as fast as he had in the past.

The Twin Peaks truce is just one of the dramatic changes in the way Linux is made and distributed that have taken place during the past few years. The phenomenon that Torvalds kicked off as a student at the University of Helsinki in 1991 had long been a loosey-goosey effort, with little structure or organization. Young students and caffeine-jazzed iconoclasts wrote much of the code in their spare time, while the overtaxed Torvalds stitched in improvements almost single-handedly.

TURNING PRO

Today, that approach is quaint history. Little understood by the outside world, the community of Linux programmers has evolved in recent years into something much more mature, organized, and efficient. Put bluntly, Linux has turned pro. Torvalds now has a team of lieutenants, nearly all of them employed by tech companies, that oversees the development of top-priority projects. Tech giants such as IBM, Hewlett-Packard, and Intel are clustered around the Finn, contributing technology, marketing muscle, and thousands of professional programmers. IBM alone has 600 programmers dedicated to Linux, up from 2 in 1999. There's even a board of directors that helps set the priorities for Linux development.

The result is a much more powerful Linux. The software is making its way into everything from Motorola cell phones and Mitsubishi robots to eBay servers and the NASA supercomputers that run space-shuttle simulations. Its growing might is shaking up the technology industry, challenging Microsoft Corp.'s dominance, and offering a new model for creating software. Indeed, Torvalds's onetime hobby has become Linux Inc. "People thought this wouldn't work. There are just too many people and companies to hang together. But now it's clear it does work," says Mark Blowers, an analyst at market researcher Butler Group.

Not that this Inc. operates like a traditional corporation. Hardly. There's no headquarters, no CEO, and no annual report. And it's not a single company. Rather, it's a cooperative venture in which employees at about two dozen companies, along with thousands of individuals, work together to improve Linux software. The tech companies contribute sweat equity to the project, largely by paying programmers' salaries, and then make money by selling products and services based on the Linux operating system. They don't charge for Linux itself, since under the cooperative's rules, the software is available to all comers for free.

POWER MOVE

Organizations don't need a rigid hierarchy to be successful. With no CEO or headquarters, and with a sprawling, decentralized structure, the Linux operating system has become so popular that it now is considered Microsoft's number one threat.

How do companies benefit from free software? In several different ways. Distributors, including Red Hat Inc. and Novell Inc., package Linux with helpful user manuals, regular updates, and customer service, and then charge customers annual subscription fees for all the extras. Those fees range from $35 a year for a basic desktop version of Linux to $1,500 for a high-end server version. The dollars can add up. Red Hat, which employs 200 programmers, is expected to see profits triple, to $53 million, in its current fiscal year, as revenues surge 56 percent, to $195 million.

Those numbers are dwarfed by the winnings for computer makers that sell PCs and servers preloaded with Linux. IBM, HP, and others capitalize on the ability to sell machines without any up-front charge for an operating-system license, which can range up to several thousand dollars for some versions of Windows and Unix. At HP, sales of servers that run the Linux operating system hit nearly $3 billion during the past fiscal year, almost double the tally of three years ago.

In the Linux community, this kind of red-meat capitalism is combined with the sharing philosophy of the open-source movement. Dick Porter, a T-shirted coder who often works under an apple tree in his garden in Wales, is on the same team as Jim Stallings, a hard-charging ex-Marine who travels the world making deals for IBM. What they have in common is a keen interest in making Linux ever more capable. The result is a culture that's cooperative and meritocratic—and Darwinian at the same time. Any company or person is free to participate in Linux Inc., and those with the most to offer win recognition and prominent roles. "Linux is the first natural business ecosystem," says James F. Moore, a senior fellow at the Berkman Center for Internet & Society at Harvard Law School.

POWER MOVE

In the digital age, companies are discovering that giving stuff away for free can actually be quite lucrative. Red Hat, for instance, has built a business around selling products and services that support Linux's free operating system.

STRANGE GROUND

To understand the inner workings of Linux Inc., *BusinessWeek* took a journey through this fast-evolving ecosystem. The unusual trip included everything from sitting in on gritty developer meetings to interviewing dozens of tech executives and engineers from Germany to China. One stop was Torvalds's home, just south of Portland, Oregon. The 34-year-old moved from Silicon Valley last summer, in part because he was hired by the Beaverton (Oregon) Linux advocacy group Open Source Development Labs Inc. He spent several hours talking about Linux as his three towheaded daughters played nearby. Something of a rock star in techie circles, he was preparing for a flight to Los Angeles for the premiere of *Shark Tale*—which was animated on Linux computers—and was taking along his oldest daughter, Patricia, then seven years old.

What's clear from these interviews is that the organization supporting Linux has matured more dramatically than most outsiders realize. While Torvalds remains at its center, he has ceded some control and accepted lots of help, thanks to some prodding from individual programmers like McVoy and some coaxing from tech giants whose fortunes have become inextricably linked with Linux. One important step was the move by IBM, Intel, and others to set up OSDL as the focal point for accelerating Linux adoption.

Perhaps most surprising, the legal attacks on Linux over the past year have unified the community. There continue to be some internal tensions—for instance, Linux backers fret that different versions of the software will become incompatible with one another. Yet a suit by SCO Group Inc., a software company that claims that IBM handed some of SCO's intellectual property to Linux, gave Linux aficionados the motivation to coordinate their efforts as never before. Tech companies have opened their checkbooks to pay for administrative support, including a legal staff that scans every stitch of code to make sure it can bear patent scrutiny. Even Linux's original idealists, who have grumbled at times about the corporatization of the community, put their complaints on hold and rallied to defend their baby. The SCO suit against IBM is slated for trial late this year.

Put it all together, and Linux has become the strongest rival that Microsoft has ever faced. In servers, researcher IDC predicts that Linux's market share based on unit sales will rise from 24

> **POWER MOVE**
>
> One reason why the Linux operating system is of such high quality is that the culture is meritocratic. People don't have to curry favor with bosses to get good assignments. Anyone can work on Linux. Those with the best ideas are the ones who rise into positions of clout.

percent today to 33 percent in 2007, compared with 59 percent for Windows—essentially keeping Microsoft at its current market share for the next three years and squeezing its profit margins. That's because, for the first time, Linux is taking a bite out of Windows, not just the other alternatives, and is forcing Microsoft to offer discounts to avoid losing sales. In a survey of business users by Forrester Research Inc., 52 percent said that they are now replacing Windows servers with Linux. On the desktop side, IDC sees Linux's share more than doubling, from 3 percent today to 6 percent in 2007, while Windows loses a bit of ground. IDC expects the total market for Linux devices and software to jump from $11 billion last year to $35.7 billion by 2008.

In response, Microsoft has launched a counterattack against what it calls its number one threat. The software giant's "Get the Facts" publicity campaign claims that Windows is more secure and less expensive to own than Linux. Microsoft has notched some victories. The city government of Paris, for instance, decided in October against a complete switchover to Linux, citing the costs of such a change. Now that Linux distributors are charging more for subscriptions, Microsoft figures that it can use the same cost-benefit arguments that helped bury old rivals, such as Netscape Communications Corp. "It's getting to be much more like the old world instead of the new world for us, and we know how to compete with that kind of phenomenon," says Microsoft chief executive Steve Ballmer.

But Ballmer may have a tough time persuading customers that Windows is cheaper than Linux. It often isn't. With Windows, end users pay an up-front fee that ranges from several hundred dollars for a PC to several thousand for a server, while there's no such charge for Linux. The total cost over three years for a small server used by 30 people, including licensing fees, support, and upgrade rights, would be about $3,500 for Windows, compared with $2,400 for a Red Hat subscription, say analysts. The situation in which Microsoft can have an edge is when a company is already using Windows. Then, in some cases, it can be cheaper to upgrade to a newer version of Microsoft's software, rather than replacing it with Linux—once you take into account the retraining expenses. Analyst George Weiss of market researcher Gartner Inc. says that Microsoft may trumpet those individual cases, but "there's no study that says Windows will be a better total cost of ownership in general."

Microsoft isn't shying away from brass-knuckles tactics in an effort to win this battle. Several sources say that its executives have been warning corporations that they're taking a legal risk by using Linux. A spokesperson for one company whose CEO met with Ballmer says that the implication of their conversation was that Microsoft is considering suing outfits that use the software and claiming that it infringes Microsoft patents. Although legal experts doubt that Microsoft would actually sue its own customers, Linux supporters say that such warnings are an effort to spread doubt and uncertainty. "Our friends in Redmond [Washington] are rattling their swords. They're trying to scare people into not switching from Windows to Linux," says Jack Messman, CEO of Linux distributor Novell. Microsoft acknowledges discussing legal risks with customers but denies trying to intimidate them. It won't say whether it believes Linux infringes on its patents.

> POWER MOVE
>
> As Linux proves, it's possible—and highly profitable—for competitors to find common ground and collaborate. IBM and Hewlett-Packard, for example, are working together on Linux, as each recognizes that a high-quality open-source system can boost both companies' bottom lines.

COMMUNAL IMPULSES

That Linux is more than holding its own against Microsoft's onslaught suggests that it could become a model for others in the tech industry. Otherwise fierce competitors—think IBM and

Hewlett-Packard—are demonstrating that they can benefit from embracing the open-source philosophy of sharing work. By collaborating on the operating system, they all get a stable foundation on which to build tech projects and save millions in programming costs. "Much software will be developed this way. It's especially good for infrastructure—stuff that affects everybody," says Torvalds. "In the long run, you can't sanely compete with the open-source mentality."

Linux Inc. has become so mature that it's clear that it could continue to thrive even without Torvalds. Already Torvalds's chief lieutenant, Andrew Morton, shares leadership duties and makes all the public appearances. From 1997 to 2003, when Torvalds worked for chip maker Transmeta Corp., putting out Linux wasn't even his full-time job—yet its market share in servers rose from 6.8 percent to 24 percent. Plus, this isn't the army: programmers don't wait around for orders. Linux's legions know how the development process works, and they just do it. "I manage people, but not in the traditional sense," says Torvalds. "I can't say, 'You do this because here's your next paycheck.' It's more like we know what we want to do, but we don't know how to do it. We try directions. Sometimes somebody disagrees and has a vision. They go and sulk in their corner for a year. Then they come back and say, 'I'll show you it's much faster if you do it this way.' And sometimes they're right."

This mix of commercial and communal impulses has its roots in the early days of personal computing. Academics and corporate researchers originally shared many of their software innovations. But that started to change in the 1980s as the industry took shape. In response, programmer Richard Stallman launched the Free Software movement. His answer: the GNU operating system, modeled on Unix, to be shared by a community of programmers. It was Torvalds who came along with a piece of software called the kernel, which is the control center of the operating system and coordinates the work of other pieces, such as the software that tells the printer to produce a page. Programmers called the kernel "Linux," a contraction of Linus and Unix, and Linux caught on as the name for the whole thing.

Torvalds decided that the group's mascot should be a friendly penguin, named Tux, partly because a pint-size Fairy penguin once nibbled his finger at an Australian zoo.

The beauty of having a nonhierarchical operation is that people don't wait for management to tell them what to do. They feel empowered and just do what is necessary to get the job done.

Stallman is still an evangelist for free software, but with his wild long hair and odd behavior, he doesn't fit in with the suit-and-tie crowd. He doesn't even speak to Torvalds anymore— since Torvalds decided to use a piece of software that wasn't open-source to help develop Linux. "The place he wants to lead people is a mistake. It isn't to freedom," says Stallman of Torvalds. During speaking engagements, Stallman often adopts the persona of "St. IGNUcius," donning a robe and a halo made of a computer disk. Chris Wright, a young programmer for OSDL, recalls a group dinner at a restaurant where the trade group hosted Stallman. Wright was impressed with Stallman's beliefs but put off by his style. "He wanted to taste everybody's food, so it was a little awkward," says Wright.

Torvalds proved to be just the guy to lead the Linux charge. He was only a casual programmer in 1991 when he started writing software to run on a PC. But after he posted the first Linux code on the Internet for others to contribute to, he got the knack for spotting quality and handling the flow of fixes. Gradually, he developed a support organization of volunteers.

Begun as a meritocracy, Linux continues to operate that way. In a world where everybody can look at every bit of code that is submitted, only the A+ stuff gets in, and only the best programmers rise to become Torvalds's top aides. "The lieutenants get picked—but not by me," explains Torvalds. "Somebody who gets things done and shows good taste— people just start sending them suggestions and patches. I didn't design it this way. It happens because this is the way people work naturally."

One reason that Linux Inc. bears little resemblance to a traditional company is that Torvalds has almost nothing in

POWER MOVE

While many managers still insist that face time is essential to running a business, Linux demonstrates that this isn't the case. A virtual organization with workers scattered across the globe, it is run by a virtual leader, Linus Torvalds, who rarely meets colleagues in person. "It's a long-distance mind-meld," says a coworker.

common with the classic hard-driving, autocratic tech-industry leaders. He rarely appears in public and largely lets other people set priorities for development. Once others come up with improvements, he shepherds them along. "Linus has power, but he doesn't have it by fiat," says Havoc Pennington, a Linux contributor who works for Red Hat. "He has power because people trust him. As long as he keeps making good decisions, people won't take it away from him."

Yet for all of his seeming passivity, Torvalds is a strong leader. He stays scrupulously neutral, never taking one company's side over another's. He focuses on the open-source development process. There, he demands high-quality work. Things must be just so, with the least amount of coding. As a result, Linux has few errors that can be exploited by virus writers. That gives it an edge on Windows, which has become a favorite target of hackers—largely because it's so widely used, but also because it has vulnerabilities that Linux doesn't. "He has set a compelling vision and inspired people to follow it," says Larry Augustin, a venture capitalist at Azure Capital Partners and an OSDL board member: "It's leadership by example, rather than leadership by hype."

Even today, Torvalds operates in a virtual world of e-mails and Web sites. He works almost entirely from a roomy house that sits on a wooded Oregon mountaintop and is decorated with taxidermic specimens, including a piranha and a crocodile. He gets up early, making strong cups of coffee for himself and his wife, Tove, a former karate champion in Finland. Then he settles in for hours of reviewing code and snapping off e-mail messages in his basement office. It's lined with science fiction and fantasy books, including classics such as *Dune* and the *Wheel of Time* series. In the afternoon, he coasts down the hill on his bicycle to a quaint village, stops at a Peet's coffee shop for a latte or Chai tea, and pumps back up the hill. Then he returns to his computers.

Although Torvalds is physically near his comrades at OSDL, he almost never sees them face to face. He visited the organization's office only once in his first three months in the Portland area, and he rarely meets with Morton, an Aussie who lives in Silicon Valley. "It's a long-distance mind-meld," says Morton. In a rare encounter last summer, they shook hands and made small talk at a picnic. The Linux community, Torvalds says, is like a huge spider web, or, better yet, multiple spider webs representing dozens of related open-source projects. His office is "near where those webs intersect."

The Linux development process begins and ends with the programmers. While there are still some individual volunteers and government agencies that chip in, more than 90 percent of the patches now come from employees of tech companies. Many of those workers are formerly independent aces who have been scooped up over the past few years. Some of these people simply submit code, and others, called maintainers, are in charge of improving specific functions.

POWER MOVE

Perhaps nothing is more demoralizing (and destructive) than working for a business where cronyism is rampant. Linux doesn't have that problem, in part because Torvalds doesn't simply talk about fairness. He leads by example, never playing favorites or kowtowing to the powerful.

From there on, it's a continuous cycle. Individuals submit patches; maintainers improve them. Then they're passed off to Torvalds and Morton, who review the patches, ask for improvements, and update the kernel. Every four to six weeks, Torvalds releases a new test version so that thousands of people around the world can probe it for flaws. He puts out a major upgrade every three years or so. Unlike at traditional software companies, there are no deadlines. The Linux kernel is done when Torvalds decides it's ready.

Linux Inc. is a series of concentric circles radiating out from Torvalds. In the first circle, you have Open Source Development Labs. The top tech companies with a stake in Linux—including HP, IBM, and Intel—have technical people on the board of directors. The board sets priorities, such as getting Linux running better for huge data centers and desktop PCs. In addition, the board is responsible for raising $10 million to protect customers from potential intellectual-property claims.

TAKING THE SUBWAY

The second circle is a dozen or so Linux distributors. Spearheaded by Red Hat and Novell, this group also includes such regional players as Red Flag Software in China and MandrakeLinux in Europe. They pick up the latest version of the kernel about once a year and package it with 1,000 or so related open-source programs, including the GNOME graphical user interface, the Firefox browser, and the OpenOffice desktop application suite.

The distributors race one another to be the first out with Linux updates, but their engineers spend most of their time on projects that they share with everybody else. For example, Novell employs open-source pioneer Miguel de Icaza, who is both a Novell vice president and the leader of the Mono project—software for building applications to run on Linux. The 34-year-old Mexican coordinates 25 Novell employees plus more than 300 other programmers, many of whom work for other tech companies. So far, de Icaza says, there have been no conflicts. His explanation: "Cooperating gets you further along than screwing your neighbor."

These Linux companies have little in common with their brethren from the dot-com boom. They're typically frugal. Matthew J. Szulik, CEO of Red Hat, takes the subway rather than a cab when he visits customers in New York and Boston. And rather than being motivated by big money, Linux programmers say that their goal is making Linux an ever-bigger force in computing. Red Hat's Pennington doesn't covet expensive wheels, proudly pointing to his 2001 Toyota Corolla in the parking lot, which he jokes is "fully loaded."

For his part, Torvalds has been amply rewarded for his role, but he's no Bill Gates billionaire. OSDL pays him a salary of nearly $200,000. In addition, he sold initial public offering shares that he got as gifts from a couple of Linux companies, including VA Linux Systems. That helped him afford his house and put money away for his daughters' educations.

POWER MOVE

Like many great products, Linux's strength lies in its adaptability. It was designed to be the Swiss Army knife of operating systems, with the ability to run everything from small networks at neighborhood copy shops to mega-Web sites like Google.

ALL-PURPOSE SYSTEM

In Linux society, there's no bowing and scraping before the rich and powerful. Executives and product managers at HP, IBM, Intel, and Oracle don't even try to pressure Torvalds and Morton to further their interests. Instead, their input goes through their engineers, who, as members of the open-source community, submit patches for the kernel or other pieces of Linux software.

The tech powerhouses have learned to play by new rules. You can't meet in private, come up with new features, and then drop massive changes on Torvalds. A handful of companies, including Intel and Nokia Corp., learned this lesson the hard way when they went about making Linux capable of running telecom gear. About two dozen of their engineers worked on the "carrier-grade" Linux project, and then, in late 2002, they posted hundreds of thousands of lines of code on a Web site. The response: outrage. "We were offended by the whole process," says Alan Cox, a top kernel programmer. The posting was quickly removed.

Still, the cultures of open-source and commercial software are melding together. Red Hat used to scatter employees around the world, the typical open-source approach. Now the company brings its workers together so that young programmers can cross-pollinate with gray-haired veterans. It works. Not only did 46-year-old Larry Woodman bond with 26-year-old Rik van Riel

POWER MOVE

To consistently create high-quality products, organizations have to be willing to take their time, not rushing an item to market before it is ready. Before a new update is released by Linux, the code is rigorously reviewed and tested by thousands of programmers worldwide. Only after corrections are made and Torvalds is fully satisfied is the product released.

by teaching him how to drive a car, but the two are working in tandem on improvements to memory management in Linux. "We complement each other," says Woodman.

These collaborations are turning Linux into an all-purpose operating system. It's secure enough that Lawrence Livermore National Laboratory loads it not only on desktop and server computers but also on the supercomputers that it uses to simulate the aging of nuclear materials. "Linux is definitely more secure than Windows," says Mark Seager, the lab's assistant department head for advanced technology. "There aren't as many ways to break the system." With the latest improvements, Linux now works on servers with more than 128 processors and can run the largest databases. The newest versions also have features, such as power management, that make them more suitable for laptop PCs.

Linux is so solid that staid corporate purchasers are adopting it aggressively for run-the-company applications. Holcim Ltd., the Swiss cement giant, just switched from Unix to Linux for some of its accounting, manufacturing, and human resource applications. The attraction: 50 percent savings on hardware and 20 percent on software. "It was a no-brainer to go with Linux," says Carl Wilson, chief operations manager for the company's North American data center.

Cost isn't the only reason that companies are switching to Linux. The data processor Axciom Corp. recently shifted some servers to the operating system, after using Unix in the past. Alex Dietz, the company's chief information officer, says that he's thinking about replacing the Windows operating system with Linux on the company's desktop computers. One important reason: Axciom doesn't want to be too dependent on Microsoft.

"[Linux] has an innate guarantee that you won't be held hostage," says Dietz.

Torvalds takes tremendous satisfaction in seeing his baby grow up. "It's like a river. It starts off a bouncy small stream and turns into a slower-moving big thing," he says.

Indeed, Linux Inc. has emerged as a model for collaborating on software development in a new way, which could have reverberations throughout the business world. Its essence is captured in one of the mottoes of the open-source world: give a little, take a lot. In a business environment where efficiency rules, that's a potent formula—maybe even strong enough to knock mighty Microsoft down a peg.

THE PROBLEM

Convincing the best minds at rival firms to collaborate to create a superior product that will be given away for free

Entering a market dominated by a Goliath that has virtually unlimited resources and is known for squashing competitors

THE SOLUTION

Give competitors a powerful financial incentive to cooperate—the ability to sell pricey products and services that will make the freebies more useful to consumers.

Win the public's confidence by maintaining high standards. Thoroughly scrutinize and test every new product and make fixes before allowing new items to be marketed and sold.

Enable a virtual organization to be productive by setting clear priorities, but giving people the autonomy to reach goals in their own way.

SUSTAINING THE WIN

Continue to inspire people to be creative and self-starting by valuing results, not face time.

LINUS
TORVALDS

LINDEN LAB:
MY SECOND LIFE—
VIRTUAL WORLD, REAL MONEY?

POWER PLAYERS

This is a journey into a place in cyberspace where thousands of people have imaginary lives. Some of them even make a good living. Big advertisers are taking notice.

Robert Hof's 2006 cover story takes readers inside Second Life.

LESSON PLAN

Develop new, more cost-effective methods of collaborating and communicating with colleagues, using multiplayer online games.

Capture consumers' attention and strengthen the brand by promoting it in the increasingly popular virtual world.

Use the online game as an "idea lab," a place to stimulate and nurture new business ideas.

Build a new revenue stream by buying and selling imaginary products in Second Life, a game that uses a currency that can be converted into real dollars.

A VIRTUAL WORLD

As I step onto the polished wood floor of the peaceful Chinese country house, a fountain gurgles softly and a light breeze stirs the scarlet curtain in a doorway. Clad in a stylish blue-and-purple dress, Anshe Chung waves me to a low seat at a table set with bowls of white rice and cups of green tea. I'm here to ask her about her booming land development business, which she has built from nothing two years ago to an operation of 17 people around the world today. As we chat, her story sounds like a classic tale of entrepreneurship.

Except that I've left out one small detail: Chung's land, her beautifully appointed home, the steam rising from the teacups—they don't exist. Or rather, they exist only as pixels dancing on the computer screens of people who inhabit the online virtual world called Second Life. Anshe Chung is an avatar, or onscreen graphic character, created by a Chinese-born language teacher living near Frankfurt, Germany. And the sitting room in which Chung and my avatar exchange text messages is just one scene in a vast online diorama operated by Second Life's creator, Linden Lab of San Francisco. Participants launch Second Life's software on their personal computers, log in, and then use their mice and keyboards to roam endless landscapes and cityscapes, chat with friends, create virtual homes on plots of imaginary land, and conduct real business.

REAL BUCKS

The avatar named Anshe Chung may be a computerized chimera, but the company she represents is far from imaginary. Second Life participants pay "Linden dollars," the game's currency, to rent or buy virtual homesteads from Chung so that they have a place to build and show off their creations. But players can convert that play money into U.S. dollars, at about 300 to the real dollar, by using their credit card at online currency exchanges. Chung's firm now has virtual land and currency holdings worth about $250,000 in real U.S. greenbacks. To handle rampant growth, she just opened a

10-person studio and office in Wuhan, China. Says Chung's owner, who prefers to keep her real name private to deter real-life intrusions: "This virtual role-playing economy is so strong that it now has to import skill and services from the real-world economy."

Oh, yes, this is seriously weird. Even Chung sometimes thinks she's tumbled down the rabbit hole. But by the time I visited her simulated abode in late February, I already knew that something a lot stranger than fiction was unfolding, some unholy offspring of the movie *The Matrix*, the social networking site MySpace.com, and the online marketplace eBay. And it was growing like crazy, from 20,000 people a year ago to 170,000 today. I knew I had to dive in myself to understand what was going on here.

As it turns out, Second Life is one of the many so-called massively multiplayer online games that are booming in popularity these days. Because thousands of people can play at once, they're fundamentally different from traditional computer games, in which one or two people play on one PC. In these games, typified by the current number one seller, *World of Warcraft*, from Vivendi Universal's Blizzard Entertainment unit, players are actors such as warriors, miners, or hunters in an endless medieval-style quest for virtual gold and power.

POWER MOVE

The popularity of multiplayer online games is yet more evidence that increasingly, consumers want to create media, not just passively watch them. And companies that tap into that desire can reap handsome rewards. Estimates suggest that roughly 10 million people fork over $15 or more a month to play these games.

All told, at least 10 million people pay $15 and up a month to play these games, and maybe 20 million more log in once in a while. Some players call *World of Warcraft* "the new golf," as young colleagues and business partners gather online to slay orcs instead of gathering on the green to hack away at little white balls. Says eBay Inc. founder and chairman Pierre M. Omidyar, whose investing group, Omidyar Network, is a

POWER MOVE

Because Second Life allows users to create any kind of virtual object from scratch and sell these objects for virtual currency convertible into U.S. dollars, players can earn real profits buying and selling in this world. One player owns "real estate" valued at $250,000. Another earns $1,900 a week selling animation programs that enable two characters in the game to dance or cuddle.

Linden Lab backer: "This generation that grew up on video games is blurring the lines between games and real life."

Second Life hurls all this to the extreme end of the playing field. In fact, it's a stretch to call it a game because the residents, as players prefer to be called, create everything. Unlike in other virtual worlds, Second Life's technology lets people create objects like clothes or storefronts from scratch, LEGO-style, rather than simply plucking avatar outfits or ready-made buildings from a menu. That means that residents can build anything they can imagine, from notary services to candles that burn down to pools of wax.

PROPERTY RIGHTS YIELD PROFITS

You might wonder, as I did at first, what's the point? Well, for one thing, it's no less real as a form of entertainment or personal fulfillment than, say, playing a video game, collecting matchbook covers, or building a life list of birds you've seen. The growing appeal also reflects a new model for media entertainment that the Web first kicked off: Don't just watch— do something. "They all feel like they're creating a new world, which they are," says Linden Lab chief executive Philip Rosedale.

Besides, in one important way, this virtual stuff isn't imaginary at all. In November 2003, Linden Lab made a policy change unprecedented in online games: it allowed Second Life residents to retain full ownership of their virtual creations. The inception of property rights in the virtual world made for a thriving market economy. Programmer Nathan Keir in Australia, for example, created a game played by avatars inside Second Life that's so popular that he licensed it to a publisher, which will soon release it on video game players and cell phones. All that has caught real-world investors' attention, too. On March 28, Linden Lab raised a second, $11 million round of private financing, including new investor Jeff Bezos, CEO of Amazon.com Inc.

Virtual worlds may end up playing an even more sweeping role—as far more intuitive portals into the vast resources of the entire Internet than today's World Wide Web. Some tech thinkers suggest that Second Life could even challenge Microsoft Corp.'s Windows operating system as a way to create entertainment and business software and services more easily. "This is why I think Microsoft needs to pay deep attention to it," Robert Scoble, Microsoft's best-known blogger, recently wrote.

WEAK SPOT

A lot of other real-world businesses are paying attention. That's because virtual worlds could transform the way they operate by providing a new template for getting work done, from training and collaboration to product design and marketing. The British branding firm Rivers Run Red is working with real-world fashion firms and media companies inside Second Life, where they're creating designs that can be viewed in all their 3D glory by colleagues anywhere in the world. A consortium of corporate training folks from Wal-Mart Stores, American Express, Intel, and more than 200 other companies, organized by learning and technology think tank The MASIE Center in Saratoga Springs, New York, is experimenting inside Second Life with ways for companies to foster more collaborative learning methods. Says Intel Corp. learning consultant Brent T. Schlenker: "We're trying to get in on the front end of this new workforce that will be coming."

POWER MOVE

The creativity unleashed by these games can spur new business opportunities offline. One player created a game within the game that was so popular with players that a game publisher paid five figures for the license and is releasing it as a game.

The more I kept hearing about all this, the more I knew that this was wa-a-a-ay more than fun and games. So early this year I signed up at www.secondlife.com, downloaded the software, logged on, and created my persona. As reporter "Rob Cranes," I embarked on my journey.

And promptly got lost in the vast, uncharted terrain.

Click: I land at the Angry Ant, a nightclub holding a "Naked Hour," where avatars in various stages of undress are dancing lasciviously. Is it getting warm in here?

Click: I stumble upon someone teaching a class on how to buy and sell virtual land to a motley crew of avatars sitting attentively on chairs watching PowerPoint slides. Do we get a toaster when we're done?

Click: Suddenly, I'm underwater at Cave Rua, watching a school of fish swim by. Cool, but what do I do here?

Click: Here's a virtual doctor's office, where a researcher runs a simulation of what it's like to be a hallucinatory schizophrenic. A menacing British voice from a TV urges: "Shoot yourself. Shoot them all. Get the gun out of the holster and shoot yourself, you !@#&!" Yikes, where's that teleport button?

My disorientation points up one of the big challenges of these virtual worlds, especially one as open-ended as Second Life: with nothing to shoot and no quest to fulfill, it's hard for newbies to know what to do. Virtual worlds require personal computers with fairly advanced graphics and broadband connections and users with some skill at software. "The tools are the weak spot," says Will Wright, legendary creator of *The Sims* video game, who nonetheless admires Second Life. For now, he says, "That limits its appeal to a fairly hard-core group."

Still, there's no denying the explosion of media, products, and services produced by users of these virtual worlds. IGE Ltd., an independent online gaming services firm, estimates that players spent about $1 billion in real money last year on virtual goods and services at all these games combined, and predicts that this could rise to $1.5 billion this year. One brave (or crazy) player in the online game *Project Entropia* last fall paid $100,000 in real money for a virtual space station, from which he hopes to earn money by charging other players rent and taxes. In January inside Second Life alone, people spent nearly $5 million in some 4.2 million transactions, buying or selling clothes, buildings, and the like.

That can add up to serious change. Some 3,100 residents each earn a net profit on an average of $20,000 in annual revenues, and that's in real U.S. dollars. Consider the story of Chris Mead, aka "Craig Altman," on Second Life. We exchange text messages via our keyboards at his shop inside Second Life, where he hawks ready-made animation programs for avatars. It's a bit awkward, all the more so because as we chat, his avatar is exchanging tender caresses with another avatar named "The Redoubtable Yoshimi Muromachi." Turns out she's merely an alter ego he uses to test his creations. Still, I can't help but make Rob Cranes look away.

POWER MOVE

In a fragmented media world, it's tough to get and hold people's attention. Games users, however, tend to become engrossed in the worlds inside these games. As a result, traditional marketers are going virtual. Coke, for instance, recently sponsored a concert inside Second Life.

THE RISKS IN A VIRTUAL ECONOMY

Mead is a 35-year-old former factory worker in Norwich, England, who chose to stay home when he and his working wife had their third child. He got on Second Life for fun and soon began creating animations for couples: when two avatars click on a little ball in which he embeds the automated animation program, they dance or cuddle together. These animations take up to a month to create. But they're so popular, especially with women, that every day he sells more than 300 copies of them at $1 or less apiece. He hopes the $1,900 a week that he clears will help pay off his mortgage. "It's a dream come true, really," he says. "I still find it so hard to believe."

His story makes me want to venture further into this economy. Besides, my photo editor is nagging me to get a shot of my avatar, which needs an extreme makeover. Time to go shopping! First I pick out a Hawaiian shirt from a shop, clicking on the image to buy it for about 300 Lindens, or about a dollar. Nice design but too tight for my taste, so I prowl another men's shop for a jacket. I find something I like, along with a dark gray blazer and pants. As a fitting finishing touch for a reporter, I add a snazzy black fedora, though I'm bummed that it can't be modified to add a press card.

I'm also feeling neglectful for leaving my avatar homeless every time I log out. It's time to buy some land, which will give me a place to put my purchases, like a cool spinning globe that one merchant offered cheap. And maybe I'll build a house there to show off to friends. I briefly consider buying a whole island, but I have a feeling our T&E folks would frown on a $1,250 bill for imaginary land. Instead, I purchase a 512-square-meter plot with ocean view, a steal for less than two bucks. Plopping my globe onto my plot, I take a seat on it and slowly circle, surveying my domain. My Second Life is good.

I soon discover that Second Life's economy has also begun to attract second-order businesses like financial types. One enterprising character, whose avatar is "Shaun Altman," has set up the Metaverse Stock Exchange inside Second Life. He (at least I think it's a he) hopes it will serve as a place where residents can invest in developers of big projects like virtual golf courses. In a text chat session in his slick Second Life office, Altman concedes that the market is "a bit ahead of its time. I'm sure it will take quite some time to build up a solid reputation as an institution." No doubt, I'm thinking, especially when the CEO is a furry avatar whose creator refuses to reveal his real name.

Premature or not, such efforts are raising tough questions. Virtual worlds may be games at their core,

POWER MOVE

Those who enter these games intending to make money, however, need to recognize the risks. The imaginary world—and their financial activities— isn't regulated, which could permit unscrupulous behavior, like money laundering or theft.

but what happens when they get linked with real money? (For one thing, people such as Chung's owner start to take changes in their world very seriously. She recently threatened to create her own currency inside Second Life after the Linden dollar's value fell.) Ultimately, who regulates their financial activities? And doesn't this all look like a great way for crooks or terrorists to launder money?

Beyond business, virtual worlds raise sticky social issues. Linden Lab has rules against offensive behavior in public, such as racial slurs or overtly sexual antics. But for better or worse, consenting adults in private areas can engage in sexual role playing that, if performed in real life, would land them in jail. Will that draw fire from law enforcement or, at least, publicity-seeking politicians? Ultimately, what are the societal implications of spending so many hours playing, or even working, inside imaginary worlds? Nobody really has good answers yet.

My head hurts. I just want to have some fun now. It's time to try Second Life's most popular game. *Tringo* is a combination of bingo and the puzzlelike PC game *Tetris*, where you quickly try to fit various shapes that appear on a screen into squares, leaving as few empty squares as you can. I settle in on a floating seat, joining a dozen other competing avatars at an event called Tringo Money Madness @Icedragon's Playpen— and proceed to lose every game. Badly. I start to get the hang of it and briefly consider waiting for the next *Tringo* event until I see the bonus feature: a movie screen showing the band Black Sabbath's 1998 reunion tour.

Instead, I seek out *Tringo*'s creator, Nathan Keir, a 31-year-old programmer in Australia whose avatar is a green-and-purple gecko, "Kermitt Quirk." It turns out that Keir's game is so popular, with 226 selling so far at 15,000 Lindens a pop, or about $50, that a real-world company called Donnerwood Media ponied up a licensing fee in the low five figures, plus royalties. *Tringo* soon will grace Nintendo Co.'s Game Boy Advance and cell phones. "I never expected it at all," Keir tells me, his awe evident even in a text chat clear across the world.

He's working on new games now, wondering if he can carve out a living. That would be even cooler than the main benefit so far: making his mum proud.

TALENT BANK

After all my travels around Second Life, it's becoming apparent that virtual worlds, most of all this one, tap into something very powerful: the talent and hard work of everyone inside. Residents spend a quarter of the time they're logged in, a total of nearly 23,000 hours a day, creating things that become part of the world, available to everyone else. It would take a paid 4,100-person software team to do all that, says Linden Lab. Assuming that those programmers make about $100,000 a year, that would be $410 million worth of free work over a year. Think of it: the company charges customers anywhere from $6 to thousands of dollars a month for the privilege of doing most of the work. And make no mistake, this would be real work were it not so much fun. In *Star Wars Galaxies*, some players take on the role of running a pharmaceutical business in which they manage factory schedules, devise ad campaigns, and hire other players to find raw materials—all imaginary, of course.

POWER MOVE

Increasingly, major corporations are finding that these virtual worlds can offer a new, cost-effective way to get work done. A British marketing firm, for instance, uses Second Life as a design studio and meeting place, saving money on air travel and creating physical models.

All this has some companies mulling a wild idea: why not use gaming's psychology, incentive systems, and social appeal to get real jobs done better and faster? "People are willing to do tedious, complex tasks within games," notes Nick Yee, a Stanford University graduate student in communications who has studied online games extensively. "What if we could tap into that brainpower?"

In other words, your next cubicle could well be inside a virtual world. That's the mission of a secretive Palo Alto

(California) start-up, Seriosity, backed by venture firm Alloy Ventures Inc. Seriosity is exploring whether routine real-world responsibilities might be assigned to a custom online game. Workers who are having fun, after all, are likely to be more productive. "We want to use the power of these games to transform information work," says Seriosity CEO Byron B. Reeves, a Stanford professor of communications.

THE FALLOUT FROM A DEREGULATED WORLD

Whether or not their more fantastic possibilities pan out, it seems abundantly clear that virtual worlds offer a way of testing new ideas like this more freely than ever. "We can and should view synthetic worlds as essentially unregulated playgrounds for economic organization," notes Edward Castronova, an associate professor in telecommunications at Indiana University at Bloomington and author of the 2005 book *Synthetic Worlds: The Business and Culture of Online Games*.

POWER MOVE

Because these games are so entertaining and involving, some experts believe that employers could use them to get workers to collaborate on projects. Tasks that are tedious offline could become interesting and engrossing if they were turned into an online game, with multiple players contributing.

I get a taste of the lack of regulation just as we're about to go to press. Logging in to Second Life after a few days off, I see that someone has erected a bunch of buildings on my avatar Rob Cranes's land, which is located in a region called Saeneul. The area was nearly empty when I arrived, but now I'm surrounded by Greek temples under construction. So much for my ocean view. Online notes left by one "Amy Stork" explain that the "Saeneul Residents Association" is building an amphitheater complex, and "your plot is smack bang in the middle." She's "confident that we can find a *much* better plot for you than this one. . . . Love, Amy xx."

Oh, really? For some reason, this causes Rob Cranes to blow a gasket. He resists my editor's advice to "head to the virtual gun store," but he fires off angry e-mail complaints to Ms. Stork and Linden Lab and deletes the trespassing buildings, planting some trees in their place. Then he reconsiders: maybe a ramshackle cabin with a stained sofa and a sun-bleached Chevy up on blocks would be a great addition to his plot.

At first, I wonder why I (or my avatar) have such a visceral reaction to this perceived intrusion. Then a flush of parental pride washes over me: my avatar, which so far has acted much like me, hanging back from crowds and minding his punctuation in text chats, suddenly is taking on a life of his own. Who will my alter ego turn out to be? I don't know yet. And maybe that's the best thing about virtual worlds. Unlike in the corporeal world, we can make of our second lives whatever we choose.

MONDAY MORNING...

THE PROBLEM
Figuring out the business applications for a new medium and technology so that the organization continues to grow and works more efficiently

Boosting the company's profits by tapping into the flourishing market economy in the virtual world

THE SOLUTION
Follow the lead of other tech-savvy companies and use the game's 3D technology to create product designs, thereby reducing the expense and time of building physical models.

Enhance communication and cooperation among teams scattered in remote locations by doing and sharing work in the virtual world.

"Play" the game for real profits. Invent innovative fictitious products and services to sell in the virtual world, and if they prove popular, create a real version to sell offline.

Take advantage of the medium's ability to transfix and absorb. Advertise a brick-and-mortar or Internet company in Second Life, and boost its visibility with a sophisticated, global audience.

SUSTAINING THE WIN
Continue to explore business opportunities offered by games, but exercise prudence, as the virtual world is largely unregulated and could become vulnerable to unsavory types.

LINDEN LAB

YANG YUANQING:
LENOVO IS CHINA'S FIRST
GLOBAL CAPITALIST

POWER PLAYER

Lenovo Group was created in 1984 as Legend Group, one of China's first capitalist enterprises. It became the world's third-largest PC player when it bought IBM's PC operation in 2005. Today it is run by Yang and CEO William Amelio, a former Dell executive.

This 2006 Global Business story by Steve Hamm and Dexter Roberts profiles China's new breed of multinational.

LESSON PLAN

Boost brand awareness abroad by seizing promotional opportunities that will give the company an international platform.

Successfully blend two corporations by recognizing the assets of each of them and figuring out ways to capitalize on those assets.

Aggressively advocate for changes that can help make the company a global leader, but do so diplomatically so as to achieve employee buy-in.

Ensure the company's long-term success by committing to R&D projects that could yield breakthrough products, even if they are costly.

115

On a bright September afternoon, a black Mercedes S320 pulls up to a curb in the middle of Beijing's bustling Zhongguancun, the consumer-electronics shopping district. Out steps a man in a conservative gray suit, with ink-black hair, a round face, and wire-rim glasses. He still has the same youthful appearance he had 18 years earlier when, as a shy, bean-thin science student, he first arrived in this neighborhood. Then called Swindler's Alley, the area was a disreputable bazaar for knockoffs and black-market software. Now all that has been replaced by neon, steel, and glass.

Yang Yuanqing, 42, chairman of Lenovo Group Ltd., the leading PC company in China, steps into the Ding Hao Electronics Mall and a dizzying scene. Everywhere there are signs, lights, and swarms of shoppers. Strolling from one shop to another to peruse the displays of his company's devices, Yang, introduced by his handlers, speaks quietly with shopkeepers. But each time he stops, he is immediately surrounded by a scrum of people giddily snapping his picture with tiny digital cameras and camera phones. Yang is a rock-star executive here, a Chinese Bill Gates.

It was in this neighborhood in 1988 that Yang began working for Lenovo—then a tiny company called Legend Group—in a nondescript three-story building. Yang slips back into the Mercedes and is soon gliding past the spot where he once bunked with four roommates in a company dormitory. Looking around, he realizes that the building has been demolished to make way for a parking lot. "Everything has been torn down," marvels Yang. "It's a total changeover."

Yang himself has undergone no less startling a transformation. He grew up poor in Hefei, a backwater city in eastern China, during the Cultural Revolution. Today he leads the world's third-largest PC company, with $13 billion in revenues. He's a rich globe-trotter: his compensation last year topped $2 million. He has a luxury apartment overlooking New York's Central Park and a home in suburban Beijing. In July, Yang moved his family to his apartment in Raleigh, North

Carolina, near Lenovo's headquarters, for a few weeks so that his kids could soak up American culture at summer camp. The Forbidden City meets Piggly Wiggly.

Last year, when Lenovo bought IBM PC Co., Yang stepped onto the world stage. He became the first Chinese executive to lead the takeover of an iconic Western business. In one swoop, he took on the world's leading technology companies. Now, as China's first truly global capitalist, he has a chance to help his homeland shed its image as a cheap manufacturing hub.

But Yang Yuanqing may turn out to be much more. From the moment he was tapped at age 29 to shake up the struggling PC unit of Lenovo's predecessor company, Yang has defied the stereotype of a Chinese manager. (That's assuming that most American business managers can name even one leader of a Chinese company.) Today he is emerging as the first of a hybrid class of leader, marrying the drive and creativity of Western management with the vast efficiencies of China's manufacturing operations.

If your idea of a Chinese boss is a cautious bureaucrat propped up by the state, Yang is not that guy. He presides over a merit-based culture built on the Silicon Valley blueprint: in an elder-worshipping country, he fearlessly promotes young people and fires employees who aren't up to snuff. He demands that people learn from their mistakes, and he's relentless about self-improvement. When it became clear 18 months ago that he was being hindered by his scant knowledge of English, he hired a tutor, watched CNN obsessively, and went from halting to conversant within a year.

Some of Yang's management techniques would make Jack Welch proud. Shortly after rising to power at

POWER MOVE

Like many top-notch business leaders, Yang Yuanqing recognizes that too many formalities can alienate management from staff. So Yang insisted that all employees be called by their given names (rather than by some lofty title). To drive home his message, he had executives, wearing signs with their names on them, stand outside the building in the morning and greet employees.

POWER MOVE

When one large company buys another, there is always the risk that more conflict than synergy will result. Lenovo avoided that pitfall when it bought IBM PC by playing on both companies' strengths. It relied on IBM's expertise in selling to large clients in the United States, while revamping IBM's manufacturing supply chain to mirror Lenovo's more efficient China operations.

Legend, he decided that managers needed to reconnect with their staff. Too many of them had highfalutin titles with the equivalent of "president" in them; Yang wanted everybody addressed by their given name. To make the point, he ordered executives to stand outside the building every morning and greet workers, while holding signs with their names written on them. "After two weeks, the change finally stuck," recalls Wang Xiaoyan, who is currently Lenovo's senior vice president for information services.

The pressure on Yang is intense, and not just from shareholders. In the summer of 2005, a few months after the IBM deal closed, Chinese Premier Wen Jiabao paid a visit to Lenovo's Beijing offices. Yang showed him the latest PCs and cell phones. As the short visit wrapped up, Wen told Yang: "You carry the hopes of China on your shoulders," according to someone who was there.

But Yang is discovering just how hard it will be to translate success in China into success everywhere else. The honeymoon after the IBM PC purchase is long over. This spring, Yang ran into a buzz saw of Beltway politics when congressional concerns about security forced the State Department to change the way it used some of the 14,000 PCs it had ordered from Lenovo. Responding to worries that Chinese government snooping technology could be tucked into the machines, the department redirected some of them to less sensitive projects.

There has been plenty of friction inside Lenovo, too. Last December, Yang and the board pushed out his second-in-command, former IBMer Steve Ward, in part because he was too slow to cut costs. Ward's replacement as CEO is the frenetic William J. Amelio, who formerly ran Asian operations for Dell Inc.

It's an oddball management setup. Yang runs the company, and Amelio reports to him, but they share a lot of responsibilities for overseeing this sprawling organization on a near-equal basis. Lenovo sells products in no fewer than 66 countries and develops them at labs in China, the United States, and Japan. Yang and Amelio also must mix the best people and traits of the old Lenovo with those of IBM. In essence, they're blending two national cultures and, to add to the stress, three corporate ones, since Amelio has been replacing some of the top executives from Lenovo and IBM with his own team, mostly from Dell. Rarely if ever has a corporate leader had to manage such a tangled web of relationships.

Yang answers to an odd mix of shareholders that includes public investors, the Chinese Academy of Sciences, the company's founders, and IBM. Each constituency has its own ax to grind. Private equity investors have a lot of clout, having sunk $350 million into the company for a 10 percent stake. Board members William O. Grabe of General Atlantic and James G. Coulter of Texas Pacific Group early on pressed for faster cost cutting and more decisive decision making. "This is an unusual melding of what had been a Chinese company, IBM, and some very strong-willed U.S. investors," says Coulter.

Yang's strategy is ambitious. Over the next couple of years, he wants to boost Lenovo's already dominant 35 percent market share in China while expanding to other emerging markets. In the West, he taps IBM for help in selling to large corporations. But for small and midsize businesses, Lenovo is now mimicking its China strategy and offering a new line of PCs through a host of retailers. Meanwhile, the company is retooling the old IBM PC Co. manufacturing supply chain to make it as efficient as Lenovo's China operations. "We want to extend the business model that was so successful in China out across the world," Yang says.

POWER MOVE

Lenovo was the tech sponsor of the Turin and Beijing Olympic Games for a simple reason: publicity. If a company wants to be a global brand, it needs to give itself a high profile on the international stage.

In the long term, Yang aims to turn Lenovo into a high-profile global brand. He took the first huge step in 2004 when he inked a deal with the International Olympic Committee to be the tech sponsor of the Turin and Beijing Olympic Games. After the merger was completed, he challenged company engineers to come up with a string of hit products for businesses and consumers worldwide in advance of the Beijing event.

At the same time, Lenovo is weaning customers off the IBM brand, which it has the right to use for five years. First, it stopped using the IBM name in advertising. Now it's gradually shifting the branding on ThinkPad laptop computers to remove IBM and replace it with Lenovo.

Former IBM engineers say that things have changed for the better since the merger—and in ways that you might not expect. Yang has kept research and development spending constant as a percentage of revenues. But because more of the work is being done in China, where engineers cost one-fifth what they do in the United States, he gets more bang for the buck. He has also dedicated 20 percent of his R&D budget for cutting-edge ideas. Under U.S. management, the unit had become focused largely on cost cutting. "It used to be, 'Can we save a penny?' Now it's, 'What new ideas do you have?'" says David Hill, executive director for corporate identity and design. One novel concept already has come from the Beijing engineers: NovaCenter, a living room–style combination of PC and TV that's now selling in China. In addition to Microsoft's Windows, it has an entertainment-oriented operating system that was created by Lenovo.

POWER MOVE

For a company to succeed on the international stage, it must devote resources to innovation. Yang rejects shortsighted penny pinching and dedicates 20 percent of his R&D budget to developing promising new ideas.

For all its big plans and lofty ambitions, though, Lenovo remains in a precarious position. Sales are still strong in China, which is expected to be one of the fastest-growing markets in coming years. However, Lenovo is up against companies several times its size. Dell alone has sunk $16 billion into Chinese factories and suppliers over the past year—more than Lenovo's worldwide sales. Lenovo's sales declined by 9 percent in the United States last quarter, signaling that the company is struggling in its efforts to build a global brand. Analysts are troubled by that report, although they expect efficiencies and revenue growth to click in over the long term. The stock (which doesn't trade on U.S. exchanges) is priced at around HK$3.30, having zigzagged between $2 and $4 for three years. In September, Lenovo was dropped from the Hong Kong Exchange's Hang Seng Index because of slack trading volumes.

Other Chinese business kingpins are watching closely to see if Yang stumbles. With a domestic economy growing at 10 percent per year and foreign reserves topping $1 trillion soon, they are hungrily eyeing attractive overseas takeover targets—everything from oil to consumer electronics. But China's early forays into global expansion have been frustrating. Electronics maker TCL Corp.'s 2004 joint venture with France's Thomson, which owns the famed RCA brand, has bled cash, resulting in shuttered plants and offices. And in 2005 an $18.5 billion bid by CNOOC Ltd. for Unocal never got off the ground; the U.S. Congress put the kibosh on it. Many Chinese executives want to see how Yang does before they, too, plunge into globalization.

Edward Tian, a friend of Yang's and former vice chairman of telecommunications giant China Netcom Group, explains how others view the Lenovo executive: "In China there's an old saying, 'Don't be the first one to eat the crab.' It's difficult to get the meat out, and you might be poisoned. People see Yuanqing as the guy eating the crab. They're waiting to see if he'll survive."

If Lenovo fizzles, it won't be for lack of intensity. Former IBMers agree that the pace of business and decision making has picked up since Yang took over. That's visible in the massive third-floor atrium of the Lenovo

POWER MOVE

When buying up a blue chip, as Lenovo did, it's critical to make the transition to the new brand name gradually so as not to scare off customers. Lenovo first stopped using the IBM name in ads, and recently, it's begun replacing IBM's name with Lenovo on ThinkPads.

Building in Beijing's sprawling Shangdi Information Industry Base, where a huge billboard with a map of China is divided into 18 sales regions. Across the bottom are columns showing the sales and ranking of each region. Every day at 7:30 p.m., the totals are tallied and messages go out to all of the managers' mobile phones. If a region comes in with less then 100 percent of its quota, its manager must immediately produce a plan for turning things around.

Sometimes Yang seems obsessed with details. Before formal dinners, he personally reviews seating arrangements to make sure all protocols are being followed. Last year, during a ceremony launching a summer camp program for kids at Lenovo Beijing, he noticed that the Lenovo flag was attached upside down on a flagpole. To get the attention of the events team, he docked their performance bonuses.

Figuring out exactly what role Yang should play in the company has been tricky. He engineered the IBM acquisition, yet during the transition he seemed to fade into the background. Ward became the company's front man with the Western press and analysts. Although Ward and Yang deny that there was ever any tension between them, one industry bigwig recalls that when he had dinner with the two a few months after the deal closed, Ward did nearly all of the talking. "It was really an uncomfortable situation," he says.

Initial encounters between Yang and Amelio were also tense. No wonder: they had been head-to-head competitors in the China market. Amelio recalls their first awkward one-on-one session at a Hong Kong hotel: "Here we were, two guys who have been trying to slit each other's throats, talking about doing something together."

At their second meeting, Yang surprised Amelio by pulling out a single sheet of paper listing the roles for Lenovo's chairman and CEO. His job included setting corporate and technology strategy and communicating with investors. Amelio's main task was running the PC business day to day. This is not the typical split between chairman and CEO—Yang would be much more hands-on, like a co-CEO. Amelio went along without complaint.

"I was surprised that he agreed so quickly," says Yang. "He looked at it for three minutes and said, 'OK.'"

Now they're a tag team. Yang goes deep on his specialties, which include marketing and distribution. Last July, for instance, he spent two days in Stuttgart, brainstorming with a dozen European salespeople about how to radically make over the way the company plans and prices products in Central Europe. Elements of the new program were launched within two weeks. Longtime IBMer Robert Pasquier, now Lenovo's distribution director for Central Europe, was impressed that Yang was willing to get his hands dirty. He says the company has been transformed culturally since Lenovo took over: "There's more of a sense of urgency with everyone. It used to be we felt pressure only at the end of the year, but now we feel it every month. People want to win."

POWER MOVE

How do two business leaders change from fierce foes into close partners? Yang and Amelio are able to work together because they divvied up duties and powers clearly and equally, so that each enjoys his own sphere of influence at the company.

Amelio, meanwhile, concentrates on fine-tuning the supply chain. "Bill often calls me boss, but I don't want to put myself only in the boss position," says Yang. "I want to contribute more to the company at all levels." Still, Yang's influence has grown over the past year. Shortly after the IBM PC takeover, the board created a powerful strategy committee headed by Yang but packed with other strong voices, including company cofounder Liu Chuanzhi. At first, the committee met monthly; now, it meets just once a quarter. "Today, Yang is the guy who runs the strategy and sets the agenda," says General Atlantic's Grabe.

A confident Yang has emerged as more of a public figure in the West. And he has become more outspoken. Yang was irate during the dustup over the State Department computer order. "We are not a government-controlled company," he insisted in a phone call placed to a *BusinessWeek* reporter shortly after the matter came to a head. "The Chinese PC market used to be dominated by state-owned enterprises. We beat them all." Today, the state-run Chinese Academy of Sciences holds 27 percent of Lenovo's shares, thanks to its early $25,000 investment in Legend. (That compares with 35 percent for public shareholders, 15 percent for employees, 13 percent for IBM, and 10 percent for private investors.) But the academy has no members on the board, and the company insists that it exerts no influence.

Later, Yang made his case directly to Congress on a sweep through Capitol Hill. Last June, at a business conference in San Francisco, he switched name tags at a table so that he could sit next to C. Richard D'Amato, a member of the congressional advisory committee that had raised the security concerns. D'Amato says that he was impressed with Yang's earnestness, but "nothing really changed my thinking."

Yang was more successful in brokering a deal to help rein in PC software piracy in China. Microsoft had been struggling for years to get Chinese computer users to pay for software, yet most of them still bought PCs that didn't include Windows and later loaded illegal copies onto their machines. In July 2005, during a meeting at Microsoft headquarters in Redmond, Washington, Gates and Microsoft chief executive Steven A. Ballmer asked Yang for help with piracy, and, over the next few months, Yang worked out a deal with Microsoft China executives. They agreed to give him a rebate on Windows and marketing help in exchange for him agreeing to load it on most Lenovo PCs sold in China. Yang gambled that other Chinese makers would follow suit, and, thanks to pressure from the government, they did. Microsoft's sales of Windows shipped on PCs in China have tripled since the deal came together last fall. Says Ballmer: "Yuanqing made a huge difference. He was willing to go out on a limb."

But if Yang is more of a risk taker than one might expect of a person who grew up in a communist state, his style is also highly calculated. Lenovo colleagues who have spent evenings

> **POWER MOVE**
>
> One key reason for Yang's success is that he takes risks—but after only much careful consideration. He studies the situation and makes a big bet only if he assesses his chances of winning as good.

with Yang playing Tuolaji, a Chinese card game, say that he studies his cards for a long time before making a move. Even when he is dealt a bad hand, he tries to figure out a way to win. They see parallels in how Yang runs the company: he's willing to take risks, but only if he has thoroughly studied a situation and figures that he has a reasonable chance of prevailing.

It's no mystery where these traits come from. Yang recalls his parents as tough taskmasters who demanded that he study hard and rank at the top of his classes. Both were surgeons, yet in 1960s China they were paid the same as manual laborers and were repeatedly sent to the countryside for reeducation and community service.

That forced Yang to grow up fast. Starting at age eight, he cooked meals for himself and two younger siblings over a smoky coal fire on the balcony of the brick housing project where the family lived in a cramped apartment. Yang's only toy was a bag of marbles; if he wanted to play ball, he'd scrunch up a cast-off cigarette package. His mother, Wang Biqin, gave him a tiny allowance each month, but he rarely spent it because he knew that she might have to take it back to buy food. Yang knew nothing of the outside world. "It was a tragedy, but it was also lucky," he says, looking back. "If you don't know what's going on outside, you don't know what you're missing."

Contrast hardscrabble Hefei in the 1960s with Yang's life today. In August he moved his parents, wife, and three children into a Raleigh apartment inside a gated community amid rolling, wooded countryside. On a steamy summer day, the Yangs gather excitedly in the living room around a low glass table spread with fresh fruit and cookies—which the children don't touch. Yang proudly prompts his eldest boy, Yang Yiqi, 11, to list the three goals he had been assigned when he went off to American summer camp. They were: learn English, make new friends, and excel at sports. "And did you reach your target?" Yang asks. The boy's enthusiastic answer: "Yes, I did!"

When asked what Yang was like when he was growing up, his father, Yang Furong, launches into a long tale that makes the whole family chuckle knowingly. Yang studied ferociously for

POWER MOVE
Buying an established overseas brand and using its name is a quick way for a firm to gain credibility abroad. However, it can be expensive, and it carries significant risks, especially if the brand hasn't been wildly successful in the first place.

the national university entrance exams. One evening, he accompanied the rest of the family on a rare outing to a movie theater, but when the house lights came up at the end, they discovered that his seat was empty. In mid-movie, he had raced back home to study.

As a teenager, Yang loved reading literature and writing poetry, but he pursued a computer science degree at university on the advice of a professor friend of his parents. Six years later, he was studying in Beijing to finish up his master's degree in computer science and was headed for an academic career when he spotted an ad for a job at Legend in a newspaper. At the time, it was a 100-person company that sold Sun Microsystems and Hewlett-Packard computers at retail. Yang signed on as a salesman at one of the few truly market-driven companies in all of China. His pay: $30 a month.

It was a fortunate choice. Legend's chief executive, Liu, had emerged in the 1980s as one of modern China's first real entrepreneurs. He and 10 other researchers at the science academy formed the company in 1984. Legend had a rocky first few years, but by the time Yang landed there, it seemed to be on solid footing. He excelled as a salesman, and Liu eventually put him in charge of small businesses and then of the company's crucial engineering workstation unit. There, he got to know Americans who worked for Sun and HP, and he scarfed up every bit of knowledge he could about how to run a successful business.

A pivotal moment came in 1994. Liu was laid up in a Beijing hospital suffering from exhaustion and stress. Legend had begun selling its own PCs in 1990, but when China opened its market to direct imports by foreign PC giants, it was caught in a pincer. As a publicly held company, Legend did not receive government support like state-owned PC outfits. Yet it didn't have the financial strength of foreign PC makers. Flat on his back for weeks, Liu used the time to consult with his underlings. He came away impressed with the youthful Yang's knowledge of the PC business and his Boy Scout–style honesty—not a small consideration at a time when Chinese enterprises were rife with corruption. Upon leaving the hospital, Liu decided to stay in PCs and create a separate division with the 29-year-old Yang in charge.

What Yang accomplished far exceeded Liu's expectations. In just three years he transformed Legend from an also-ran into the leading PC player in China. He switched from using only a direct sales force to also selling through a vast network of retailers. And he focused on innovation. Until then, the technology in PCs sold in China had been a generation behind the technology in those sold in the West. Legend shipped PCs based on Intel's new Pentium processor at the same time they were shipped in North America. Yang also opened up the now-vast consumer market with low-cost, super-easy-to-use PCs. One Legend model let PC novices set up an Internet connection with a single push of a button.

Along the way, Yang learned management lessons that would later prove vital. As the new boss of the PC Division, he supervised several of the company's founders. That was hard for them to swallow. To make matters worse, Yang didn't have a diplomatic sinew in his body. He fired half of the staff, forced managers to radically alter the way they did business, bawled out people when they screwed up, and ignored criticism. It was not very Chinese of him. Liu saw that he very nearly had a revolt on his hands, so he called a management meeting to deal with it. "I criticized Yang so severely he almost broke down in tears," recalls Liu. "But this had a good effect. . . . He started to change his work style."

POWER MOVE

Satisfying customer demand has been a key strategy of Yang's. Creating and marketing inexpensive, easy-to-use, and fast PCs to China's new computer users helped turn the company into a leading PC maker in just three years.

While Yang became more diplomatic, he remained a reformer. When the PC Division switched buildings in 1997, he used the move to break with the past. He insisted on a more formal dress code and trained all employees in phone etiquette. This is when he made everyone start referring to managers by their given names.

It wasn't until later that Legend employees understood what Yang was up to. He wanted Legend managers and employees to think and act like techies in Silicon Valley, Boston, or Berlin. Yang knew that unless Legend expanded beyond the borders of China, it would not be able to match the clout of the foreign PC giants. So, when Liu handed the CEO job to him in 2001, Yang made globalization one of his long-term goals.

His big opportunity came in 2003, when he learned that IBM was interested in selling off its large but money-losing PC unit as part of its move to services. Yang saw this deal as a way for Legend, which was about to rebrand itself as Lenovo, to leap onto the world stage without having to grind it out country by country. But the entire board of directors lined up against Yang. Think about what he was asking the Lenovo elders to do: a $3 billion company based in China would be taking over a $10 billion global behemoth. IBM had practically invented the PC industry; if Big Blue couldn't make money selling these machines worldwide, how could little Lenovo hope to do any better? "We had all built this company, and nobody wanted to take such a big risk," explains Liu.

Yang and his team dug in. They made presentation after presentation to the board until the endless meetings took on the feel of a court trial. Yang was under extreme pressure. One day, when Yang was venting to him in the locker room after a workout, his friend Tian suggested that they take a sauna to relax. Yang had something of an epiphany after the two men jumped, naked, into a pool of icy water. "Suddenly Yuanqing was not a serious person anymore. He smiled like a baby," recalls Tian. Eventually, Yang prevailed. He agreed to give up the CEO role to a more worldly Western executive and convinced the board that he could make the former IBM operations more profitable.

Today, Yang's moments of pure bliss are rare. At the end of a long workday in September, he sits at a table in the Bai Family Courtyard Restaurant in Beijing—a setting as far from the smoky balcony in Hefei as you could imagine. The restaurant is decorated in the style of Beijing's Imperial Palace, and the waitresses dress like Qing Dynasty princesses in elaborate headdresses and lavishly embroidered silk clothing. They bring dish after exquisite dish, an overabundance that seems designed to make up for the privations of China's past.

For a moment, Yang appears relaxed. But that's only temporary. A guest asks what keeps him up at night, and Yang quickly answers: almost everything. "I have a lot of anxiety dreams," he says. "It's the normal emergencies of running a company every day. A customer complains. We're not able to meet demand. There's a shortage of parts. I often wake up, and sometimes I'm up all night."

POWER MOVE

Like so many change agents, Yang has learned that fast reforms are best implemented with a soft touch. At first, Yang was so hard-driving and impolitic—chewing out staff in public and ignoring criticism—that his staff nearly mutinied.

THE PROBLEM

Continuing to grow the business in the domestic market, while also expanding abroad

Purchasing an overseas company and effectively merging its operations into yours

THE SOLUTION

Move quickly and decisively to trim costs, but not at the expense of R&D, which will keep the company innovative.

Realistically assess the skills and capabilities of both partners, and make sure to take full advantage of them.

Use the new acquisition's name on products if it will help sell them in the new market, but methodically phase out the use of that name and introduce the new brand.

SUSTAINING THE WIN

Create a leading global company by continuing to apply the best of both cultures—the energy and creativity of American enterprise and the efficiency of Chinese manufacturing.

YANG YUANQING

APOLLONIA POILÂNE AND MISA HARADA: BREAD AND FASHION LESSONS FROM EUROPE

POWER PLAYERS

The Poilâne bakery in France is run by the founder's granddaughter, who holds to tradition while carefully integrating technology—and studying at Harvard. Misa Harada has revitalized the dormant millinery business with eye-catching designs worn by TV and sports celebrities, and even by the Rolling Stones.

Amber Haq's 2007 Poilâne story and Misa Harada profile appeared in BusinessWeek Online.

LESSON PLAN

Maintain the company's reputation for excellence by holding tight to the practices that distinguish the brand.

Zealously protect the company's relationship with customers, even if that sometimes involves taking actions that will cut into profits.

Learn the trade from industry pros so that the company reflects best business practices but exploits untapped opportunities.

Give the brand prestige by nurturing ties with upscale clientele and retail outlets.

A FRENCH BREAD OBSESSION

At a time when the bottom line rules, Poilâne stands out by maintaining its commitment to high quality. The company adheres to its 75-year tradition of using stone-milled gray flour in its sourdough loaf and still relies on bakers to cut dough by hand.

This is a story about bread. But it's also a tale of a third-generation family business, a bitter fraternal rift, a tragic helicopter crash, and a young woman thrust suddenly into managing an icon of French society while completing her undergraduate studies at Harvard.

Making bread may seem like a prosaic task, but Poilâne is no mere bakery. Started in 1932 in a tiny shop near St. Germain des Près in Paris, Pierre-Léon Poilâne's storefront has grown to become a potent national symbol. The rich, dark sourdough loaves— a marked contrast to France's ubiquitous fluffy white baguettes—are the gold standard for country-style bread in supermarkets and restaurants across France. And now, under the steady hand of 23-year-old chief executive Apollonia Poilâne, some 20 percent of Poilâne's output is shipped abroad by air courier to devoted customers in New York, Johannesburg, and Tokyo.

At the same time, Poilâne maintains its handcrafted feel. Walk down a quaint street in the Left Bank and you will notice a long line of sophisticated French customers queuing in front of the original store for their daily bread and pastries. Forget low carbs or wheat-free. "Our bread is food for the body," says Apollonia Poilâne. The loaves are still shaped by hand and baked in brick-lined wood-burning ovens. Even the bread wrappers and the company's familiar logo have a tasteful and reserved quality.

BREAD IN THE BONE

It all starts with Poilâne's celebrated *miche*, or sourdough loaf, made from stone-milled gray flour, salt from the Guerande region, and a sourdough starter that dates from Apollonia's grandfather's original batches. The choice of gray flour is deliberate: after World War II, most French bakers reverted to using the refined white flour characteristic of baguettes. ("An Austrian import," Apollonia confides.) Poilâne's sourdough loaf, in contrast, retains more of the wheat's nutritional content—and keeps for a week.

The third-generation proprietor holds close to her grandfather's philosophies and business practices: using the best ingredients, attention to detail at every stage of the process, and nurturing long-term customer and supplier relationships. To that, she's now adding brand management and a growing international distribution network.

"My grandfather came to Paris from Normandy to bake," says Apollonia. "We dedicate ourselves to preserving the best of our food culture and sharing it with our customers."

SQUABBLING SIBLINGS

Apollonia recalls growing up in the shadow of her grandfather, counting loaves, distributing cookies in bags, and making figurines out of dough. But family life chez Poilâne wasn't always so idyllic. While Pierre-Léon was still running the business, his sons Max and Lionel had a huge falling out, and Max left to set up his own bakery on the south side of Paris. Lionel, Apollonia's father, took over running the original operation in 1973.

The rift never healed. The rival brother markets his nearly identical line of baked goods under the name Max Poilâne and distributes the products to supermarkets and via two bakeries in Paris. Lionel and the rest of the family sued him for trademark infringement, but lost the case when courts ruled that Max had the right to use his own name. Remarkably, Apollonia has never met her uncle and refuses to speak about

POWER MOVE

How does a company preserve the traditions that have made it great, while also expanding capacity to meet demand? It uses new technology judiciously. Poilâne can produce up to 19 metric tons of bread each day through its "manufacture," a factory that combines machinery with artisanal techniques.

the fraternal battle, although the tussle over the brand name clearly still rankles.

"I am completely dispassionate about the split," she says. "My concern is that I have clients calling me saying that they found my bread unsatisfactory. Then they realize that it's not my bread. That's an issue."

POWER MOVE

Thriving, long-lasting family businesses often have a mission that guides heirs from generation to generation. For 75 years, Poilâne's central goal has been to sell handcrafted bread that is "food for the body."

A TRAGIC TURN

After high school, Apollonia made the decision to attend college in the United States, in part because her mother, Irena, was Polish-American. Her Harvard entrance essay was on the importance of bread in her life and how she would one day run the company. "You might say that flour and not blood runs through her veins," says Geneviève Briere, Poilâne's communications manager.

But Apollonia had no idea how soon and how unexpectedly her future career would arrive. In 2002, when she was just 18, her parents were killed in a helicopter crash off the coast of Brittany. The Harvard freshman lost her family overnight and had to take charge of the family business while grappling with her grief.

Now a senior majoring in economics, Apollonia manages Poilâne's operations trans-Atlantically during the school term, returning to Paris every four to six weeks to check in. "She had always been groomed for the role, and it was understood that one day she would be running the show," says Briere.

Despite her youth, the sharp scion of the French baking dynasty is well in control. Under Apollonia's leadership, Poilâne's annual sales have grown from 11.6 million ($15

POWER MOVE

Like so many successful high-end companies, Poilâne makes sure that its products are sold primarily in upmarket institutions and nurtures these relationships.

million) in 2001 to 13.8 million ($17.9 million) last year. Though known for her decision-making skills, she relies on a team of *responsables*, many of whom worked alongside her father and have been with the company for more than 35 years.

MAKING DOUGH

Apollonia's management has already earned praise from longstanding associates of Lionel's. "Respect for the finest ingredients and a passion for artisanship were inculcated in Apollonia by her father," says Ariane Daguin, chief executive of D'Artagnan, the largest retailer of foie gras in the United States and a long-time business partner. "I admire this devotion to quality—something that is fast dying out in a market obsessed with industrial processes and production objectives."

> **POWER MOVE**
>
> For a business to grow globally, it must be willing to embrace new distribution networks. Poilâne moved online in the late 1990s, and now Internet sales account for 20 percent of its revenues.

Poilâne's transformation from local Parisian bakery to international business is largely due to Apollonia's father. When Lionel took over the business, his mission was to preserve the artisanal techniques and know-how of the past, while combining them with the best of present-day technology. "His idea of 'retro-innovation' is the cornerstone of our business success," says Apollonia. Known for hanging out with the artists and philosophers of the Left Bank, Lionel incarnated the epicurean lifestyle.

To expand the business, Lionel opened a "manufactury"— a sort of bread factory—in Bièvres, near Paris, that employs 50 bakers working round the clock to feed 24 wood-fired ovens. He also launched international distribution through third-party retailers and opened the company's first British boutique, on Elizabeth Street in London. In the last years before his death, he launched Internet sales, which now account for 20 percent of revenues.

POWER MOVE

To ensure customer satisfaction, Poilâne makes good on its promises. As a result, Apollonia has been known to turn down orders if she can't guarantee delivery (and thus fresh bread) within two days.

But even as sales surged and Poilâne became an internationally recognized brand, Lionel resisted industrializing its processes. "It would be foolish to assume that we don't use some technology to make our bread," says Apollonia. " But we hold tight to certain fundamentals. Bièvres is a 'manufactury,' not a factory, because we use hands, not machines." The dough is still cut by hand, and the "proving," or letting the dough rest under a wet cloth before baking, is done naturally. The company now produces 12 to 19 metric tons of bread per day, some 20 percent of which is destined for international markets.

BREAD IS LIFE

Today, Poilâne gets 80 percent of its sales from retail distributors, including some of the most prestigious names in the gastronomy business—Agata and Valentina in New York, Takashimaya in Japan, and the upscale Monoprix supermarket chain in France and Germany. The bread is served in restaurants such as London's Mirabelle and The Ivy. "Poilâne stayed true," states Jean-Louis Dumonet, executive chef at SnAKS at Saks in New York and Maître Cuisinier de France. "They haven't deviated from their brand. They understand that the recipe and preparation are healthy and natural, something I prize as a chef."

The thriving Internet business is Poilâne's newest means of reaching demanding customers around the world. Its global clientele includes Hollywood film stars and titans of the French entertainment industry. Apollonia says that she prefers to decline orders if delivery cannot be guaranteed within 24 to 48 hours. And although it's known that she also supplies bread to the Elysée Palace, home of French President Jacques Chirac, she won't discuss specific clients.

"In France, we have an expression, *'Le pain, c'est la vie'* (bread is life)," Apollonia says. "It's the common denominator of all civilizations, and a friend is someone you share your bread with." For 75 years, this is how Poilâne has seen its role in its customer's lives. Now, for the young woman taking charge of a French icon, bread is more than ever a family affair.

POWER MOVE

Sometimes even wildly successful family businesses vanish when the founders die. Poilâne has thrived because each generation has trained the next and has maintained a cadre of well-trained, loyal managers.

HARADA: HATMAKER TO THE STARS

Misa Harada's sense of style has always been informed by rebellion. So when the Japanese entrepreneur and hat stylist decided to launch her own business in the late 1990s, her goal was to break away from the millinery status quo and use eclectic, avant-garde design to woo a younger, more trend-conscious clientele. The result? Today, Harada is the hottest hand in hats, with designs that dress the heads of TV stars, sports figures, and even members of the Rolling Stones.

In what seemed like an anachronistic business, Harada has successfully redefined headwear fashion for a new global audience. She set up a sole proprietorship in 1998 with no external financing and booked revenues of $120,000 in the first year. Now, her sales hover just below $1 million annually, and her brand recognition is soaring internationally.

POWER MOVE

Like many successful entrepreneurs, Misa Harada studied under a master and learned the basics of the business before striking out on her own.

From rebellious student to international trendsetter, Harada has come a long way since her conservative upbringing in Japan. Born in 1968 in Nagoya, she went to London in 1987 to attend university. But her newfound freedom and the 1980s fashion scene, which married street style and punk music, fueled

Having a following among the fashion elite helps give a company an image of stylishness. Harada got her big break when she convinced a trendy magazine to feature some of her hats, and pop star Janet Jackson decided to give her a commission.

her creative energy. She dropped out of school, enrolled at the Royal College of Art, and had her first taste of hatmaking.

"CAPTURING THE ZEITGEIST"
Today, she deals in a dazzling range of styles: Trilbys in shocking pink, oversized Bakerboy caps, asymmetric cloche hats in Liberty cotton, and trimmings of silk, leather, metal buckles, or Swarovski crystal. The style is at once edgy, cool, and elegant. "Design is about capturing the zeitgeist," Harada says. "I am interested in street culture movements and in translating them into a 3-D expression you can wear."

Thrust into the real world after graduating from the Royal College of Art in 1994, Harada went to work for stylist Frederick Fox, who supplied hats to the Queen. There, she designed haute couture and commercial lines and learned the tricks of the trade, from design and materials to quality control and cost management. "Sustaining a hat business is difficult," she says. "Competition is fierce, production costs are high, and brand value is primordial."

Worse, it's not a very big market. In Britain, the number of hat designers is so small that the Employment Department doesn't even keep statistics. The U.S. Census Bureau counts 251 hat manufacturers, with retail sales totaling $978 million in 2005—most of that from baseball caps. The luxury hat market is even smaller, ever since the hat industry declined rapidly in the 1960s. But since the 1980s, it has started to come back, with annual growth of 5 to 10 percent, propelled largely by the fashion choices of entertainment industry icons.

SURPRISINGLY AFFORDABLE HEADPIECES
Harada's big break came in April 2001. She had networked heavily in the fashion world and had managed to get a series

of hats featured in *ID* magazine. Pop star Janet Jackson spotted them there and handed Harada a commission to design chapeaux for the star's upcoming world tour.

That was the catalyst for a successful entrée into the music and film industry. Harada's hats now regularly embellish the pages of magazines such as *Vogue*, *Harper's Bazaar*, and *W*, as well as showing up on the heads of characters in TV series such as *Sex and the City* and *Ally McBeal*. She has outfitted pop novelties the Scissor Sisters, and last year she won a gig to supply hats to Mick Jagger and the rest of the Rolling Stones for their most recent world tour.

Such high-profile deals have helped Harada grow annual sales at 23 percent while maintaining profit margins of around 60 percent across her collections. Yet her headpieces are surprisingly affordable, often in the range of only a few hundred dollars.

DOCUMENTARY SUBJECT

Harada remains the sole designer and retains complete control over operations, aided by a team of six managers. Her brother Shintaro runs her business in Japan. Across the company, she has tried to instill a culture that focuses on cultivating long-term relationships, maintaining high quality, and keeping costs down through advantageous purchasing deals.

But commercial success hasn't lessened the admiration Harada enjoys from the fashion world. "Misa's uncluttered, simple, sharp designs make for really interesting pieces of art, as much as they are hats," says Ian Bennett, an independent hatmaker and millinery lecturer at the Royal Academy of Art. "Being an individual is difficult in this market."

A rising star in London fashion circles, Harada enjoys even higher status in Japan, where she is considered an über-cool

POWER MOVE

Don't assume that high fashion means high-end prices. Harada built a fashionable brand by creating products that appeal to hipsters of all incomes.

fashion guru. She was recently featured in a three-month-long documentary series produced by Japanese national broadcaster TBS entitled *Zyonetsu Tairiku* (*Passion Continent*), and she has been commissioned to write a lifestyle book. Her collaboration with Japanese retailers extends to the internal rebranding of certain Japanese department stores, including Isetan, Hank-Yu, and Estnation.

To open up new markets, Harada has established women's and men's lines and recently launched a baby line, which is fast winning customers in Japan. Today, Harada puts out 300 styles in six broad collections every year. "I make hats for people who move with the times, icons of everyday life," Harada says. "Like them, I don't stick to conventions. I'm not scared of taking risks." Nor, apparently, are her loyal customers. Hats off to Harada!

MONDAY MORNING...

THE PROBLEM
Growing a high-profile, high-end, and high-profit brand in a niche industry

Branching out in new overseas markets while preserving the company's signature style

THE SOLUTION
Expand the range of goods sold, but make sure that all of them uphold company standards.

Stay in control of operations, especially the creative processes that are at the heart of the business.

Remain committed to the traditions that define the brand, whether that's creating products with all-natural ingredients or simple, artistic designs.

SUSTAINING THE WIN
Ensure the longevity of the company by investing in the training of managers and passing on a devotion to the company's mission.

APOLLONIA POILÂNE
and
MISA HARADA

ROBERT FUNK:
EXPRESS PERSONNEL'S TEMP
STRATEGY FOR PERMANENT GROWTH

POWER PLAYER
As rivals focused on executive searches, Express Personnel's Robert Funk concentrated on placing fill-in workers. Here's how his gamble paid off.

Be on the lookout for opportunities in troubled businesses.

Hold onto experienced personnel.

Concentrate on flexible, temporary hires when resources are limited.

Don't lose sight of the goal of providing jobs for many.

Stacy Perman's 2005 profile of Robert Funk appeared in BusinessWeek Online.

PERMANENT STRATEGY

It was a series of fortunate events that propelled Robert Funk, the son of a dairy farmer, from rural poverty to running a billion-dollar franchise empire. In 1965 and fresh out of college, Funk had planned on returning to tiny Duvall, Washington, to purchase his cousin's dairy farm. His cousin, however, wasn't quite ready to sell, telling him to get a job and return in two years.

So Funk, who had earned a master's in business administration and theology from Seattle Pacific University, turned to ACME Personnel Services, a professional staffing outfit. ACME placed him at the Seattle office of financial-data giant Dun & Bradstreet, where he handled credit reports.

Funk didn't care much for the job, and when he left it three months later, he told ACME that he was better suited to helping people than to pulling companies' credit reports. As it turned out, ACME was impressed with Funk and offered him a position at its Oklahoma City headquarters. His cousin decided not to sell the farm, and Funk stayed at ACME for nearly 20 years.

GAMBLING MAN

When ACME's president died unexpectedly in 1983, Funk, who by then had become a vice president, teamed up with two partners and decided to buy 6 of the firm's 84 franchises. It was a gamble: not only was this a period of economic instability, but ACME was on the verge of bankruptcy. "It was the worst recession since the dust bowl," he says. "And we barely had enough for the payroll the first year."

Convinced that he could transform the outfit, Funk mortgaged his house and 20 acres of land outside Tulsa and plowed all of his savings into the business. Then he borrowed another $150,000 from a local bank. In the early days, he kept overhead low by having

> **POWER MOVE**
>
> Like many entrepreneurs, Robert Funk found success in part because he was willing to make a big bet when a great opportunity came along. When the president of ACME died, Funk mortgaged his house and tapped his savings to buy up six franchises.

his wife, Nedra, handle all accounting and bookkeeping. And instead of downsizing, Funk retained the experienced staff— a considerable financial expense, but with it came dedication and loyalty that he credits for the company's survival.

In a strategic move that Funk now calls "fortuitous," while most of his competitors continued to focus on executive recruitment, his newly named Express Personnel Services decided to concentrate on flexible, temporary hires. Funk hired a marketing team to get out and sell the concept. "That was counterintuitive," he says. "In a recession, it's usually the sales and marketing people that are the first to be let go."

POWER MOVE

Just because industry giants have written off certain sectors doesn't mean that others couldn't turn those sectors into profitable niches. Express has grown to be a $1.3 billion company by concentrating on serving small and midsized clients.

SCREENING RESOURCE

The venture took off, bringing in $2 million in revenue in its first year. The following year, Funk purchased the rights to 30 ACME franchises across the country. Today, Funk presides over an Oklahoma City–based professional-staffing company with some 500 offices in the United States, Canada, South Africa, and Australia. Last year, Express registered $1.3 billion in revenue and placed nearly 300,000 people.

Funk, who also owns the Oklahoma Blazers hockey team and Express Ranches, one of the nation's largest cattle breeders, says that he takes his business philosophy from motivational sales guru Zig Ziglar. "If you help enough people, the money runs to the door," he says. "We are in this to help people— and we've succeeded. We've found hundreds of thousands of people jobs, and with franchises we've helped people to have their own businesses."

Now the sixth-largest staffing firm in the United States, behind industry leader Manpower, privately held Express keeps growing by continually recruiting and interviewing potential hires to expand its already-deep database and supply talent on

It's not enough to simply articulate a mission for the organization. The mission needs to be one that will resonate and inspire people. Express's mission:"We are in this to help people."

short notice. "Because of our expertise, in a bad economy, we become a real screening resource," Funk says. "And in a good economy, we know how to recruit when there is a shortage of talent."

SHIFTING POOL

Sales jumped 30 percent in 2004, according to Funk, and Express rolled out 58 new locations. By 2009, he expects his business to double to 900 locations and hit $2 billion in revenue.

The tectonic shifts that have hit the American workforce in recent years through layoffs and outsourcing, as well as an increasingly mobile labor pool that is interested in flexibility, have meant that more companies and potential hires are turning to staffing firms.

According to the Bureau of Labor Statistics, 9 out of 10 businesses now use the services of a staffing-industry firm, with more than one-third of those surveyed saying that they plan to increase the practice. And the American Staffing Association reports that temporary-job placement has been increasing 10 percent annually over the past seven years. In 2003, the employment-staffing industry earned $63.3 billion, with the vast majority—$56 billion— coming from temporary staffing.

FLEXIBILITY'S APPEAL

Express provides temporary and permanent staff in the professional, clerical, and light-industry sectors. Unlike some competitors, it focuses mostly on placements in small and midsized outfits. In addition, it offers clients a range of value-added services. "We realized that most of these

Frequently, people who buy troubled businesses will try to rein in costs by slashing staff. But by holding on to experienced staff, Express made it through the tough times and also gained employees' dedication.

companies don't want to deal with the time and expense of having their own HR department," Funk says. So Express provides them with a Web-based payroll service, health insurance and 401(k) administration, and benefit-consulting and legal services.

> **POWER MOVE**
>
> In a fiercely competitive economy, the companies that win are the ones that offer value-added services. Express, for instance, provides Web-based payroll, health insurance, and 401(k) administration services.

Funk encourages companies to keep 20 percent of their staffs as flexible hires, allowing them to keep a weather eye on the economy and the worth of prospective employees. If and when business picks up, temps can be switched to the permanent payroll.

How does this work in practice? As an example, Funk cites a manufacturing outfit that recently needed 30 people to work for between 6 weeks and 12 weeks. Within a half hour, Express was able to tap its inventory files and assemble a group of potential hires. During their temporary employment, all paperwork and payroll was handled by Express, reducing the burden on the manufacturing firm.

MORE THAN "WARM BODIES"

When Funk took the helm, Express was split evenly between company-owned branches and franchises. He noticed that the franchisees were much more aggressive in their marketing and earned more than their corporate counterparts. So to help the firm grow without much capital on hand, he shifted entirely to a franchise model.

Over the years, however, that strategy has grown to encompass part of Express's desire to build relationships with its customers and the communities in which it operates— efforts that are more successful in the hands of local franchisees who know their cities and towns. "It's all about relationships," Funk says.

Jean Goetz, who has operated an Express franchise with her husband, Carl, in Fort Lauderdale, Florida, for the past 14 years, maintains detailed profiles on each potential hire and meets with them personally when a job order comes in—a process that she believes provides a better match for companies. "We just don't send out warm bodies, which I notice some of our competitors do," Goetz says. "We evaluate each person."

POWER MOVE

To help grow a company that is short on cash, consider shifting to a franchise model. Express has discovered an added benefit: franchisees can enjoy deeper relationships with local communities.

NEXT MOVE

Funk, of course, has even bigger plans. "I eventually see us as number one in the United States," he says. "I'm 64. I'm old. We've got to get there more quickly than most. We'll see where we are at in 2009 and determine what it will take to get us there through internal growth. We have no plans to merge or make acquisitions."

In the meantime, he has begun franchising his cattle operations and hopes to expand the business into Eastern Europe and South America. "I guess I've gone back to my roots," he says. Robert Funk may be back on the ranch, but he's come a long way from the farm.

MONDAY MORNING...

THE PROBLEM

Taking over a business that is teetering on the edge of bankruptcy at a time when the economy is weak

Growing the business despite a lack of capital

THE SOLUTION

Figure out which segments of the market have been ignored or poorly served by competitors, and move in quickly to establish dominance in those areas.

Keep overhead as low as possible without laying off veteran staffers who can help the company navigate through the difficult transition.

Finance an expansion into new markets by relying on franchises.

Formulate a compelling vision and mission, and use it to guide the company.

SUSTAINING THE WIN

Avoid complacency by adding franchises in new markets and pushing hard to be number one in the industry.

Apply the same winning strategies that helped make the firm successful to ancillary businesses.

ROBERT FUNK

149

ROGER AND CYNTHIA LANG: FROM SILICON VALLEY TO SUN RANCH

POWER PLAYER

Former tech CEO Roger Lang and his wife aim to make their Montana ranch a thriving business—without hurting the environment.

This 2005 story by Sarah Lacy appeared in BusinessWeek Online.

LESSON PLAN

Stay committed to "doing the right thing," even though it may prove costly initially.

Branch out into promising sideline businesses that could bolster the company's fortunes.

Be willing to tap a nest egg or write off ventures as charity in order to pursue a vision.

Understand that entrepreneurs are "ideas" people, frequently selling off one business only to start the next.

PRINCIPLES INTO PRACTICE

A few years back, Roger and Cynthia Lang found themselves with a lot of money and even more free time. Roger's software company, Infinity Financial Technology, had gone public in 1996, and just two years later was acquired by SunGard Data Systems for a reported $313 million, leaving them millionaires many times over.

Like stereotypical Californians, the Langs love the outdoors and are passionate about conservation. So, with all that cash, they decided to put their principles into practice. That same year, they bought ponytailed actor Steven Segal's ranch in Cameron, Montana, and set out to prove that raising cattle could go hand in hand with environmental ideals.

"RIGHT THING TO DO"

Using some of their Silicon Valley business acumen, they also aim to make a pretty penny. "There are all kinds of conflict in the Western landscape," Roger says. "I don't know that resolving them is going to be the outcome of this experiment, but I can try. And I can make a difference at a local level."

Today the Langs preside over a miniature empire in the Treasure State. Sun Ranch is an 18,000-acre spread that raises grass-fed organic beef. Adjacent Papoose Creek Lodge is a luxury travel outpost, and their Madison Bend complex a mile down the road includes a general store and lower-price cabins.

POWER MOVE

Creating a perfectly "green" business can require an infusion of cash and yield scant profits, at least in the short term. In fact, the Langs see some of their projects as philanthropic.

On top of all that, the Langs have donated almost 7,000 acres to the Nature Conservancy of Montana and are doing several ecologically friendly side projects—like building a hatchery for indigenous trout. "I don't think we'll make money on that, but I also think it's the right thing to do," Roger says. "Some of our projects are more philanthropic than business-related."

COWGIRL CUTICLES

Green Acres it's not, and Roger isn't exactly the Marlboro Man either. He doesn't wear a cowboy hat, chaps, or anything with a fringe, and he's uncomfortable on a horse. And like any effective CEO, he delegates much of the day-to-day activities to his ranch manager.

He's part of the local ranching group but is very up front about being a techie at heart. He even talks about his love of ranching in geekspeak. "I'm intrigued by finding sustainable equations," he says, describing how to reach compromise among ranchers, hunters, and environmentalists.

Cindy blends in a bit more. Unlike Roger, she's very comfortable in the saddle, and once she had settled into Montana, the longtime urbanite found herself dressing the part.

> **POWER MOVE**
>
> It is possible to enter a field in which you lack experience. Roger Lang felt uncomfortable on a horse when he purchased the ranching business. The key: he knows what he doesn't know and is willing to delegate.

She remembers picking up her sister at the airport the first time she visited. "I was driving a big pickup truck with filthy jeans and dirt under my nails," Cindy recalls. "She said, 'I never thought I'd see you like this!'"

WORK IN PROGRESS

It may be rare for tech CEOs to become ranchers, but it's not uncommon for "retired" entrepreneurs to find themselves running a company again. John Nesheim, who teaches entrepreneurship at Cornell University and is the author of *High Tech Startup*, likens that unquenchable entrepreneurial instinct to a young man who has just noticed girls for the first time and "is never the same again."

Most entrepreneurs are visionaries, Nesheim notes, and that quality doesn't go away simply because they cash out. "You can be at the opera, in the shower, or fishing, and—Bing! Bing! Bing!—ideas are popping into your head, and it doesn't seem to stop," he says.

> **POWER MOVE**
>
> Often, company founders move on to a new business after "retiring" or cashing out. Once they get the entrepreneurial bug, they want to pursue their next big idea.

For the Langs, the goal isn't to subsidize the Sun Ranch businesses, but to turn them into profitable, thriving operations—and do so without compromising ecological standards. It's still a work in progress. The couple purchased the local general store two years ago and have made it profitable, Roger says. The five-year-old Papoose Creek Lodge should break even this year or next.

And the ranch? It's adding a consulting division to pass on eco-friendly pointers. For example, instead of shooting wolves, his head rancher intimidates them by sleeping alongside the cattle.

The Langs are hoping that the consulting takes off; otherwise, the ranch alone isn't likely to turn a profit. It's hard to make it as a rancher these days, and Sun Ranch is no exception. Margins are thin, tracking commodity prices has become essential, and most Montana ranches simply aren't big enough to make the economies of scale work. That's why you'll often hear spokespeople for conservation groups lamenting that much of the West is disappearing beneath subdivisions and resorts.

BRAZIL RETREAT

Lang has seen ranchers exacerbate this trend by borrowing money to run more cattle in the hope of a big year, only to see themselves wiped out when prices crash.

Add to that the hidden costs of being eco-friendly. Because the Langs don't want to overgraze the land, they run fewer cattle than others might choose to do on the same acreage. And they have installed a pricey collapsible fencing system that allows migrating elk to pass through their property. These are projects that many other ranchers in the area couldn't afford to try, even if they wanted to, Roger says.

The sprawling Montana spread isn't the only project on the Langs' plate. In 2000, Roger founded Transaria, now a

50-employee business based about an hour away in Bozeman, Montana, that provides high-speed Internet access to rural communities. And once their 15-year-old son goes off to college, Cindy plans to set up a foundation for funding dance programs in California.

When they aren't in Silicon Valley or home on the range, the Langs escape to their vacation retreat in Brazil. "There are three very different Cindys," Cindy explains about her lifestyle. "The sophisticated California board member, the cowgirl, and the fun-loving, open-to-everything one in Brazil."

POWER MOVE

Sometimes ancillary services can produce more revenue than the main business. It's so difficult to make ranches profitable these days that the Langs have opened a local general store, a lodge, and a consulting division to offset losses.

FAMILY VALUES

Lest they sound like superheroes, Cindy admits that the many hobbies and business ventures come at a price. The two shuttle back and forth between Montana and California, where their primary home is located, making sure that someone is there to drive their youngest son to school every day. And when they are at the ranch or lodge, they work long days.

"My friends describe me as such a jet-setter," says Cindy. " But when I go to Montana, my day starts at six in the morning, and I don't come in until 11:30 at night. One of the challenges you face is definitely keeping a family together." As most entrepreneurs know, that's a whole different kind of conservation.

THE PROBLEM

Making the transition into a new industry in which even pros find it hard to turn a profit

Creating a lucrative business that is also environmentally sound

THE SOLUTION

Recognize that "serial" entrepreneurs are not uncommon and can find success at subsequent start-ups.

Apply business know-how to your new venture, but recognize your limitations and hire veterans to manage day-to-day affairs.

Be realistic about the costs involved in running an eco-friendly company. Analyze expenses and be careful to identify hidden costs.

SUSTAINING THE WIN

Keep following your passion for the business, but strive for balance so that work doesn't crowd out family life.

ROGER and CYNTHIA LANG

THE MYSPACE GENERATION

They live online. They buy online. They play online. Their power is growing. The youths of today have different online habits, and the young people now running the social networks can provide invaluable insights to marketers. Accessing these existing social networks with authentic communities is a better bet than attempting to build a network from scratch. But it is important to carefully weigh the risks of partnering with or acquiring a fast-growing social network, as the business model is still unproven.

A SOCIAL NETWORK

The Toadies broke up. It was four years ago, when Amanda Adams was 16. She drove into Dallas from suburban Plano, Texas, on a school night to hear the final two-hour set of the local rock band, which had gone national with a hit 1995 album. "Tears were streaming down my face," she recalls, a slight Texas lilt to her voice. During the long summer that followed, Adams turned to the Web

in search of solace, plugging the lead singer's name into Google repeatedly until finally his new band popped up. She found it on Buzz-Oven.com, a social networking Web site for Dallas teens.

Adams jumped onto the Buzz-Oven network, posting an online self-portrait (dark hair tied back, tongue out, goofy eyes for the cam) and listing her favorite music so that she could connect with other Toadies fans. Soon she was heading off to biweekly meetings at Buzz-Oven's airy loft in downtown Dallas and helping other "Buzzers" judge their favorite groups in marathon battle-of-the-bands sessions. (Buzz-Oven.com promotes the winners.) At her school, Frisco High—and at malls and concerts—she passed out free Buzz-Oven sampler CDs plastered with a large logo from Coca-Cola Inc., which backs the site in the hope of reaching more teens on their home turf. Adams also brought dozens of friends to the concerts that Buzz-Oven sponsored every few months. "It was cool, something I could brag about," says Adams, now 20 and still an active Buzzer.

Now that Adams is a junior at the University of North Texas at Denton, she's online more than ever. It's 7 p.m. on a recent Saturday, and she has just sweated her way through an online quiz for her advertising management class. (The quiz was "totally out of control," write classmates on a school message board minutes later.) She checks a friend's blog entry on MySpace.com to find out where a party will be that night. Then she starts an Instant Messenger (IM) conversation about the evening's plans with a few pals.

POWER PLAY

For teens and twentysomethings, a social network is more than just another communications medium. It's where they spend a lot of their time hanging out.

KIDS, BANDS, COCA-COLA

At the same time, her boyfriend IMs her a retail store link to see a new PC he just bought, and she starts chatting with him. She's also postering for the next Buzz-Oven concert by tacking the flier on various friends' MySpace profiles, and she's updating her own blog on Xanga.com, another social network that she uses mostly to post photos. The TV is set to TBS, which plays a steady stream of reruns like *Friends* and *Seinfeld*—Adams has a TV in her bedroom as well as one in the living room—but she keeps the volume turned down so that she can listen to iTunes over her computer speakers. Simultaneously, she's chatting with dorm mate Carrie Clark, 20, who's doing pretty much the same thing from a laptop on her bed.

You have just entered the world of what you might call Generation @. Being online, being a Buzzer, is a way of life for Adams and 3,000-odd Dallas-area youth, just as it is for millions of young Americans across the country. And increasingly, social networks are their medium. As the first cohort to grow up fully wired and technologically fluent, today's teens and twentysomethings are flocking to Web sites like Buzz-Oven as a way to establish their social identities. Here you can get a fast pass to the hip music scene, which carries a hefty amount of social currency offline. It's where you go when you need a friend to nurse you through a breakup, a mentor to tutor you on your calculus homework, an address for the party everyone is going to. For a giant brand like Coke, these networks also offer a direct pipeline to the thirsty but fickle youth market.

Preeminent among these virtual hangouts is MySpace.com, whose membership has nearly quadrupled since January 2005, to 40 million members. Youngsters log on so obsessively that MySpace ranked number 15 on the entire U.S. Internet in terms of page hits in October, according to Nielsen//NetRatings. Millions also hang out at other up-and-coming networks such as Facebook.com, which connects college students, and Xanga.com, an agglomeration of shared blogs. A second tier of some 300 smaller sites, such as Buzz-Oven, Classface.com, and Photobucket.com, operate under—and often inside or next to—the larger ones.

Although networks are still in their infancy, experts think they're already creating new forms of social behavior that blur the distinctions between online and real-world interactions. In fact, today's young generation largely ignores the difference. Most adults see the Web as a supplement to their daily lives.

POWER PLAY

Acquiring or becoming an investor in a social network can be risky. While the start-ups are growing fast—MySpace.com alone has some 40 million members—many networks haven't turned a profit, and it's not clear that they ever will.

They tap into information, buy books or send flowers, exchange apartments, or link up with others who share their passion for dogs, say, or opera. But for the most part, their social lives remain rooted in the traditional phone call and face-to-face interaction.

The MySpace generation, by contrast, lives comfortably in both worlds at once. Increasingly, America's middle- and upper-class youth use social networks as virtual community centers, a place to go and sit for a while (sometimes hours). While older folks come and go for a task, Adams and her social circle are just as likely to socialize online as off. This is partly a function of how much more comfortable young people are on the Web: fully 87 percent of 12- to 17-year-olds use the Internet, vs. two-thirds of adults, according to the Pew Internet & American Life Project.

Teens also use many forms of media simultaneously. Fifteen- to eighteen-year-olds average nearly $6^{1}/_{2}$ hours a day watching TV, playing video games, and surfing the Net, according to a recent Kaiser Family Foundation survey. A quarter of that time, they're multitasking. The biggest increase: computer use for activities such as social networking, which has soared nearly threefold since 2000, to 1 hour and 22 minutes a day on average.

Aside from annoying side effects like hyperdistractibility, there are some real perils for underage teens and their open-book online lives. In a few recent cases, online predators have led kids into dangerous real-life situations, and parents' eyes are being opened to their kids' new world.

ONE-HIT WONDERS

Meanwhile, the phenomenon of these exploding networks has companies clamoring to be a part of the new social landscape. News Corp. Chief Executive Rupert Murdoch has spent $1.3 billion on Web acquisitions so far to better reach this coveted demographic—$580 million for the July 2005 purchase of MySpace parent Intermix Media alone. And Silicon Valley venture capitalists such as Accel Partners and Redpoint Ventures are pouring millions into Facebook and other social networks. What's not yet clear is whether this is a dot-com era replay, with established companies and investors sinking huge sums into fast-growth start-ups with no viable business model. Facebook, barely a year old and run by a 21-year-old student on leave from Harvard, has a staff of 50 and venture capital— but no profits. (Note: In "The MySpace Generation" [Cover Story, December 12], *BusinessWeek* reported that Facebook.com is not profitable. A company spokesman says that Facebook has been making money since January.)

Still, consumer companies such as Coke, Apple Computer, and Procter & Gamble are making a relatively low-cost bet by experimenting with networks as a way to launch products and to embed their brands in the minds of hard-to-reach teens. So far, no solid format has emerged, partly because youth networks are difficult for companies to tap into. They're also easy to fall out of favor with: while Coke, Sony Pictures Digital, and Apple have succeeded with MySpace, Buzz-Oven, and other sites, P&G's attempt to create an independent network around a body spray, for one, has faltered so far.

Many youth networks are evanescent, in any case. Like the one-hit wonder the Baha Men (*Who Let the Dogs Out*) and last year's peasant skirts, they can evaporate as quickly as they appear. But young consumers may follow brands offline—if companies can figure out how to talk to youths in their online vernacular. Major companies should be exploring this new medium, since networks transmit marketing messages "person-to-person, which is more credible," says David Rich Bell, a marketing professor at the University of Pennsylvania's Wharton School.

POWER PLAY

Established consumer brands that want to reach the lucrative youth market are starting to try promoting their products in social networks. One reason: it's still relatively inexpensive to do so.

POWER PLAY

A social network need not have a huge community to prove valuable. If the community is small but active, it can still be a good way for marketers to target a particular demographic.

So far, though, marketers have had little luck at creating these networks from scratch. Instead, the connections have to bubble up from those who use them. To understand how such networks get started, share a blue-cheese burger at the Meridian Room, a dive bar in downtown Dallas, with Buzz-Oven founder Aden Holt. At six feet nine inches, with one blue eye, one brown one, and a shock of shaggy red hair, Holt is a sort of public figure in the local music scene. He started a record label his senior year at college and soon turned his avocation into a career as a music promoter, putting out 27 CDs in the decade that followed.

In 2000, as Internet access spread, Holt cooked up Buzz-Oven as a new way to market concerts. His business plan was simple. First, he would produce sample CDs of local bands. Dedicated Buzzers like Adams would do the volunteer marketing, giving out the CDs for free, chatting up the concerts online, and slapping up posters and stickers in school bathrooms, at local music stores, and on telephone poles. Then Holt would get the bands to put on a live concert, charging them $10 for every fan he turned out. But to make the idea work, Holt needed capital to produce the free CDs. One of his bands had recently done a show sponsored by Coke, and after asking around, he found the company's Dallas sales office. He called for an appointment. And then he called again. And again.

Coke's people didn't get back to him for weeks, and then he was offered only a brief appointment. With plenty of time to practice his sales pitch, Holt spit out his idea in one breath: marketing through social networks was still an experiment, but it was worth a small investment to try reaching teens through virtual word of mouth. Coke rep Julie Bowyer thought the idea had promise. Besides, Holt's request was tiny compared with the millions that Coke regularly sinks into campaigns. So she wrote him a check on the spot.

DEEP CONNECTIONS

By the time Ben Lawson became head of Coke's Dallas sales office in 2001, Buzz-Oven had mushroomed into a nexus that allowed hundreds of Dallas-area teens to talk to one another and socialize, online and off. A middle-aged father of two teens himself, Lawson spent a good deal of time poring over data about how best to reach youth like Adams. He knew what buzzer Mike Ziemer, 20, so clearly articulates: "Kids don't buy stuff because they see a magazine ad. They buy stuff because other kids tell them to."

What Lawson really likes about Buzz-Oven is how deeply it weaves into teens' lives. Sure, the network reaches only a small niche. But Buzzers have created an authentic community, and Coke has been welcomed as part of the group. At a recent dinner, founder Holt asked a few Buzzers their opinions about the company. "I don't know if they care about the music or they just want their name on it, but knowing they're involved helps," says Michael Henry, 19. "I know they care; they think what we're doing is cool," says Michele Barr, 21. Adds Adams: "They let us do our thing. They don't censor what we do."

POWER PLAY

Corporations and venture capitalists who invest in social networks need to be careful not to meddle with their DNA. News Corp., which bought MySpace, is trying to preserve the community by keeping creative control in the hands of its youthful founders.

Words to live by for a marketer, figures Lawson, particularly since Coke pays Buzz-Oven less than $70,000 a year. In late October, Holt signed a new contract with Coke to help him launch Buzz-Oven Austin in February. The amount is confidential, but he says it's enough for 10,000 CDs, three to four months of street promotions, and 50,000 fliers, plus some radio and print ads and a Web site promotion. Meanwhile, Buzz-Oven is building relationships with other brands such as the *Dallas Observer* newspaper and McDonald's Chipotle restaurants, which kick in free food for Buzzer volunteers who promote the shows. Profits from ticket sales are small but growing, says Holt.

Social networks often shun banner or pop-up ads. Instead, they prefer less intrusive and more subtle forms of promotion, which they say are more effective. Apple, for instance, sponsors an Apple chat group on Facebook.com.

Not so long ago, behemoth MySpace was this tiny. Tom Anderson, a Santa Monica (California) musician with a film degree, partnered with former Xdrive Inc. marketer Chris DeWolfe to create a Web site where musicians could post their music and fans could chat about it. Anderson knew music and film; De Wolfe knew the Internet business. Anderson cajoled Hollywood friends— musicians, models, actors—to join his online community, and soon the news spread. A year later, everyone from Hollywood teen queen Hilary Duff to Plano (Texas) teen queen Adams has an account.

It's becoming a phenomenon unto itself. With 20 million of its members logging on in October 2005, MySpace now draws so much traffic that it accounted for 10 percent of all advertisements viewed online during the month. This is all the more amazing because MySpace doesn't allow those ubiquitous pop-up ads that block your view, much less spyware, which monitors what you watch and infuses it with pop-ups. In fact, the advertising can be so subtle that kids don't distinguish it from content. "It's what our users want," says Anderson.

As MySpace has exploded, Anderson has struggled to maintain the intimate atmosphere that gives social networks their authenticity. When new users join, Tom becomes their first friend and invites them to send him a message. When they do, they hear right back, either from him or from one of the one-quarter of MySpace's 165 staffers who handle customer service. Ask Adams what she thinks of MySpace's recent acquisition by News Corp., and she replies that she doesn't blame "Tom" for selling; she would have done the same thing. She's talking about Anderson, but it's hard to tell at first because she refers to him so casually, as if he were someone she has known for years.

That's why Murdoch has vowed not to wrest creative control from Anderson and DeWolfe. Instead, News Corp.'s resources will help them nourish new MySpace dreams. Earlier this month, they launched a record label. In the next few months, the duo says, they will launch a movie production unit and a satellite radio station. By March they hope to venture into wireless technology, perhaps even starting a wireless company to compete with Virgin Mobile or Sprint Nextel's Boost. Says DeWolfe: "We want to be a lifestyle brand."

It's proof that a network—and its advertising—can take off if it gives kids something that they badly want. Last spring, Facebook founder Mark Zuckerberg noticed that the college students who make up most of his 9.5 million members were starting groups with names like Apple Students, where they swapped information about how to use their Macs. So he asked Apple if it wanted to form an official group. Now—for a fee that neither company will disclose—Apple sponsors the group, giving away iPod Shuffles in weekly contests, making product announcements, and providing links to its student discount program.

The idea worked so well that Facebook began helping anyone who wanted to start a group. Today there are more than a dozen, including several that are sponsored by advertisers such as Victoria's Secret and Electronic Arts. Zuckerberg soon realized that undergraduates are more likely to respond to a peer group of Apple users than to the traditional banner ads, which he hopes to eventually phase out. Another of his innovations: ads targeted at students of a specific college. They're a way for a local restaurant or travel agency to advertise. Called Facebook Announcements, it's all automated, so anyone can go onto Facebook, pay $14 a day, and fill out an ad.

POWER PLAY

Social networks hold distinct dangers for corporate advertisers. Advertisers do not have control over what users say—and one well-networked person can have a powerful voice online. Also, these networks—and the communities they support—can be ephemeral.

SPARKLE AND FIZZLE

Still, social networks' relationships with companies remain uneasy. In 2004, for example, Buzz-Oven was nearly thrown off track when a band called Flickerstick wanted to post a song called *Teenage Dope Fiend* on the network. Holt told Buzzers:"Well, you can't use that song. I'd be encouraging teenagers to try drugs." They saw his point, and several Buzzers persuaded the band to offer a different song. But such potential conflicts are one way, Holt concedes, in which Buzz-Oven's corporate sponsorships could come to a halt.

Like Holt, other network founders have dealt with such conflicts by turning to their users for advice. Xanga cofounder John Hiler has resisted intrusive forms of advertising like spyware or pop-ups, selling only the conventional banner ads. When advertisers recently demanded more space for larger ads, Hiler turned the question over to Xanga bloggers, posting links to three examples of new ads. More than 3,000 users commented pro and con, and Hiler went with the model that users liked best. By involving them, Hiler kept the personal connection that many say they feel with network founders—even though Xanga's membership has expanded to 21 million.

So far, corporate advertisers have had little luck creating such relationships on their own. In May, P&G set up what it hoped would become a social network around Sparkle Body Spray, aimed at tweens. The site features chatty messages from fake characters named for scents like Rose and Vanilla ("Friends call me Van"). Virtually no one joined, and no entries have comments from real users. "There wasn't a lot of interesting content to engage people," says Anastasia Goodstein, who documents the intersection between companies and the MySpace Generation at Ypulse.com. P&G concedes that the site is an experiment, and the company has found more success with a body-spray network embedded in MySpace.com.

The most basic threat to networks may be the whims of their users, who after all are mostly still kids. Take Friendster, the first networking Web site to gain national attention. It erupted in 2003, going from a few thousand users to nearly 20 million. But the company couldn't keep up, causing frustration among users when the site grew sluggish and prone to crash. It also started with no music, no message boards or classifieds, and no blogging. Many users jumped ship when MySpace came along, offering the ability to post song tracks and more elaborate profiles. Friendster has been hustling to get back into the game, adding new options. But only 942,000 people clicked on the site in October 2005, vs. 20.6 million who clicked on MySpace in the same period.

That's the elusive nature of trends and fads, and it poses a challenge for networks large and small. MySpace became a threat to tiny Buzz-Oven last year when Buzzers found that they could do more cool things there, from blogs to more music and better profile options. Buzzer message board traffic slowed to a crawl. To stop the hemorrhaging, Holt joined MySpace himself and set up a profile for Buzz-Oven. His network now operates both independently and as a subsite on MySpace, but it still works. Most of Holt's Dallas crowd came back, and Buzz-Oven is up to 3,604 MySpace members now, slightly more than when it was a stand-alone network.

Even if the new approach works, Holt faces a succession issue that's likely to hit other networks at some point. At 35, he's well past the age of his users. Even the friends who helped him launch Buzz-Oven.com are in their late twenties—ancient to members of his target demographic. So either he raises the age of the group—or replaces himself with someone younger. He's trying the latter, betting on Mike Ziemer, a 20-year-old recent member, even giving him a small amount of cash.

Ziemer, it turns out, is an influencer. That means that record labels and clothing brands pay him to talk up their products, for which he pulls down several hundred dollars a month. Ziemer has spiky brown hair and a round, expressive face. In his MySpace profile, he lists his interests in this order: Girls. Music. Friends. Movies.

POWER PLAY

Corporations have enjoyed more success with sponsorships and embedding their brands in networks than they have had when they tried to create a network on their own. P&G tried to build a social network around its Sparkle Body Spray. Hardly anyone joined.

167

He has 4,973 "friends" on MySpace. At all times, he carries a T-Mobile Sidekick, which he uses to text message, e-mail, and send photos to his friends. Sometimes he also talks on it, but not often. "I hate the phone," he says.

Think of Ziemer as Aden Holt 2.0. Like Amanda Adams, he's also a student at UT-Denton. When he moved to the area from southern California last year, he started Third String PR, a miniature version of Buzz-Oven that brings bands to the 'burbs. He uses MySpace.com to promote bands and chats online with potential concertgoers. Ziemer can pack a church basement with tweens for a concert, even though they aren't old enough to drive. On the one hand, Ziemer idolizes Holt, who has a larger version of Ziemer's company and a ton of connections in the music industry. On the other hand, Ziemer thinks Holt is old. "Have you ever tried to talk with him over IM?" he says. "He's just not plugged in enough."

That's exactly why Holt wants Ziemer on Buzz-Oven. He knows the younger entrepreneur can tap a new wave of kids—and keep the site's corporate sponsor on board. But he worries that Ziemer doesn't have the people skills. What's more, should Ziemer lose patience with Buzz-Oven, he could blacklist Holt by telling his 9,217 virtual friends that Buzz-Oven is no longer cool. In the online world, one powerfully networked person can have a devastatingly large impact on a small society like Buzz-Oven.

For now, the gamble is paying off. Attendance at Buzz-Oven events is up, and if the Austin launch goes smoothly, Holt will be one step closer to his dream of going national. But given the fluid world of networks, he's taking nothing for granted.

This 2005 cover story was written by Jessi Hempel, with Paula Lehman.

SOURCES

Chapter 1: Ben Elgin, with Jay Green and Steve Hamm,
"Keeping the Edge at Google," 2004;
http://www.businessweek.com/magazine/
content/04_18/b3881001_mz001.htm.

Chapter 2: Dean Foust, "All Business," 2005;
http://www.businessweek.com/magazine/content/
05_46/b3959601.htm?chan=search.

Chapter 3: Steve Hamm, with Beth Carney, "Can Pro Gaming
Go Legit?" 2005; http://www.businessweek.com/
magazine/content/05_41/b3954113.htm?chan=
search.

Chapter 4: Sarah Lacy and Jessi Hempel, "Digg.com's
New Silicon Valley Brat Pack," 2006,
http://www.businessweek.com/magazine/content/
06_33/b3997001.htm?chan=search.

Chapter 5: Stanley Holmes, "Higher Grounds at Espresso
Vivace Roasteria," Winter 2007;
http://www.businessweek.com/magazine/content/
07_09/b4023448.htm?chan=smallbiz_smallbiz+
index+page_success+stories.

Chapter 6: Dexter Roberts with Frederik Balfour, Bruce Einhorn,
Michael Arndt, Michael Shari, and David Kiley,
"China's Power Brands: Mainland Entrepreneurs
Versus Multinationals," 2004;
http://www.businessweek.com/magazine/content/
04_45/b3907003.htm?chan=search.

Chapter 7: Robert Hof, "Amazon's Risky Bet," 2006;
http://www.businessweek.com/magazine/content/
06_46/b4009001.htm?chan=search.

Chapter 8: Steve Hamm, "Linux Inc.," 2005;
http://www.businessweek.com/magazine/content/
05_05/b3918001_mz001.htm?chan=search.

Chapter 9: Robert Hof, "My Second Life—Virtual World, Real
Money?" 2006; http://www.businessweek.com/
magazine/content/06_18/b3982001.htm.

Chapter 10: Steve Hamm and Dexter Roberts, "Lenovo Is
China's First Global Capitalist," 2006;
http://www.businessweek.com/magazine/
content/06_50/b4013062.htm?chan=search.

Chapter 11: Amber Haq, "Apollonia Poilâne" and "Bread
and Fashion Lessons from Europe," 2007;
http://www.businessweek.com/
globalbiz/content/feb2007/gb20070206_625846.ht
m?chan=smallbiz_smallbiz+index+page_success+st
ories; http://www.businessweek.com/globalbiz/
content/feb2007/gb20070222_827320.htm?chan=
smallbiz_smallbiz+index+page_success+stories.

Chapter 12: Stacy Perman, "Express Personnel's Temp
Strategy for Permanent Growth," 2005;
http://www.businessweek.com/smallbiz/content/
apr2005/sb2005044_1885_sb038.htm?chan=search.

Chapter 13: Sarah Lacy, "From Silicon Valley to Sun Ranch," 2005;
http://www.businessweek.com/smallbiz/content/
jan2005/sb20050118_0575_sb038.htm?chan=
search.

TRENDS: Jessi Hempel, with Paula Lehman,
"The MySpace Generation," December 12, 2005;
http://www.businessweek.com/magazine/content/
05_50/b3963001.htm?chan=search.

CONTRIBUTORS

MICHAEL ARNDT was named editor of *BusinessWeek*'s new monthly, BW Chicago, in August, after seven years in the magazine's Chicago bureau as a senior correspondent. He has covered virtually every business beat, from pharmaceuticals and health care to manufacturing, from airlines to retail and fast food. He has also edited various sections of the magazine.

Before joining *BusinessWeek* at the start of 2000, Mr. Arndt was a business editor at the *Chicago Tribune* for five years, overseeing a staff of up to two dozen reporters and directly responsible for the paper's Sunday business section. He was chief economics correspondent for the *Tribune* in its Washington, DC, bureau from 1990 to 1995. He became a business reporter in 1987, after seven years as a metro reporter in the city and suburbs. During his career at the *Tribune*, Mr. Arndt reported from Russia, Mexico, Canada and Japan. His first job in Chicago was at the now defunct City News bureau.

FREDERIK BALFOUR is the Asia correspondent in Hong Kong for *BusinessWeek*. Prior to *BusinessWeek*, he was deputy bureau chief for Agence France Presse in Vietnam. Balfour first came to Asia in 1986 on a McGraw-Hill Correspondent's Fund Fellowship. Balfour received a special McGraw-Hill achievement award for covering the Iraq War, where he was embedded with the U.S. Army's 3rd Infantry Division. He holds a master's degree from the London School of Economics, a master's degree in journalism, and a PhD in economics from the University of California at Berkeley.

PETER BURROWS is a senior writer at *BusinessWeek,* a position he assumed in early 2007. He has been a member of the magazine's Silicon Valley bureau since 1995, covering various segments of high tech, including computers, networking and digital media. From 1993 to 1995, he was a correspondent in the Dallas bureau, covering tech and the energy sector.

BRUCE EINHORN is Asia regional editor in *BusinessWeek's* Hong Kong bureau. He was previously the Asia technology correspondent. Einhorn joined *BusinessWeek* as a Taiwan stringer in 1993. Prior to *BusinessWeek*, Einhorn was a Taiwan stringer for the *Los Angeles Times*, the Asian *Wall Street Journal*, and *Journal of Commerce*. Einhorn is a graduate of Princeton University. In 1996 and 1998 he received the Overseas Press Club's Morton Frank Award for the best business reporting from abroad.

BEN ELGIN is a correspondent for *BusinessWeek* in the San Mateo bureau. He joined the magazine in September 2000, covering Internet companies with a focus on Internet content, Net advertising, B2B exchanges, and Internet outsourcing.

Before joining *BusinessWeek*, Mr. Elgin was a senior editor and features editor at *Sm@rt Reseller* magazine from December 1997 through September 2000. He was also an associate editor for *ZDNet* from August 1996 through December 1997.

Mr. Elgin received his bachelor's in 1995 from the University of California, San Diego, with a major in communications and a minor in history.

DEAN FOUST is the Atlanta bureau chief for *BusinessWeek*, a position he has held since 1998. In this role, he oversees the magazine's coverage of all news from the eight-state Southeast, including *BusinessWeek's* coverage of such leading companies as Coca-Cola, Bank of America, and Wachovia.

Mr. Foust holds a bachelor's degree in journalism and political science from the University of North Carolina at Chapel Hill.

He received the 1998 Gerald Loeb Award for Distinguished Business and Financial Journalism with colleague Michael Mandel for their coverage of the economy. He was also a finalist for the 1995 Loeb Award with another colleague for coverage of the Federal Reserve.

JAY GREENE joined *BusinessWeek* in January 2000. He started as a member of the San Mateo, California, bureau based in Seattle. A year later, he opened the two-correspondent Seattle office and became bureau chief. In addition to overseeing the bureau, he is responsible for technology coverage in the Pacific Northwest.

Mr. Greene has been a reporter for a wide range of publications. Prior to joining *BusinessWeek*, he was the Microsoft reporter for the *Seattle Times*. He also worked as a business reporter for the *Orange County Register* in Santa Ana, California, where he covered health care. Before that, he was a film and finance reporter for *Variety* in Los Angeles, California, covering the entertainment industry. He was also a business reporter for the *Plain Dealer* in Cleveland, Ohio, the *Daily News* in Los Angeles, California, and the *Press Enterprise* in Riverside, California.

STEVE HAMM is a senior writer at *BusinessWeek* attached to the information technology team. He writes about technology, globalization, innovation, and leadership. He also writes a blog for BusinessWeek Online, Bangalore Tigers, about the offshoring of work.

He has worked for *BusinessWeek* for 10 years, starting in Silicon Valley and then moving to New York in 1999. His book, *Bangalore Tigers,* about the rise of the Indian tech industry, was published by McGraw-Hill Professional Books in 2006.

AMBER HAQ is a London- and Paris-based writer covering Design, Innovation, and European small businesses for *BusinessWeek* since 2006. Her writing extends to the arts and cultural coverage and she regularly contributes to *Newsweek International* and the *Asahi Shimbun-International*

Herald Tribune among other publications. Prior to journalism, Haq was a management consultant with Pricewaterhouse-Cooper's LLP in London. She holds an MA(Hons) in chemistry from Balliol College, University of Oxford, as well as an ACA from the Institute of Chartered Accountants of England and Wales.

JESSI HEMPEL was the Innovation department editor for *BusinessWeek*. Prior to this position, she was a staff editor, covering philanthropy, technology, and youth. Before joining *BusinessWeek*, Hempel worked for Time Asia, as well as various nonprofit organizations. Hempel is a graduate of Brown University and received a master's in journalism from the University of California at Berkeley.

ROBERT HOF is the San Mateo bureau chief at *BusinessWeek*, a position he assumed in 2002. Prior to this position, he was a senior correspondent in San Mateo, responsible for covering the semiconductor industry, telecommunications, and other technology beats. Since joining *BusinessWeek* in 1988, Mr. Hof has covered a wide range of beats, including technology, state politics, and retail and environmental issues.

Mr. Hof holds a bachelor's degree in journalism from San José State University.

STANLEY HOLMES is a correspondent in *BusinessWeek*'s Seattle bureau, responsible for coverage of companies such as Boeing, Starbucks, and Nike.

He also reports on the aerospace and defense industries and contributes to *BusinessWeek*'s annual "Best Global Brands" special report.

Mr. Holmes earned a master's degree from Columbia University's Graduate School of Journalism and a bachelor's in English from Western Washington University.

DAVID KILEY is a senior correspondent in *BusinessWeek*'s Detroit bureau, responsible for coverage of autos and marketing. Previously, he was the marketing editor for *BusinessWeek*, a post he held since July 2004. Prior to this, he was Detroit bureau chief for *USA Today,* where he primarily covered the auto industry but also wrote articles about the large Muslim population in Michigan. Mr. Kiley has held editor and reporter posts at *Adweek, Brandweek,* and CNN. He has also worked in the advertising industry, holding executive titles at Interpublic Group agency, Lowe & Partners.

Mr. Kiley is the author of two books: *Getting The Bugs Out: The Rise, Fall and Comeback of Volkswagen in America* (John Wiley & Sons, 2001) and *Driven: Inside BMW, The Most Admired Car Company in the World* (John Wiley & Sons 2004). He won the Ken Purdy Award for Excellence in Automotive Industry Journalism in 2001 for *Getting The Bugs Out.* He was elected the 2005-2006 president of the International Motor Press Association.

Mr. Kiley received his bachelor's degree from Fordham University.

SARAH LACY has been a business reporter for 10 years, most recently covering technology for *BusinessWeek.* Her book on the new generation of Internet moguls and the rise of Web 2.0 will be published by Penguin Publishing in 2008.

PAULA LEHMAN is an editorial assistant at *BusinessWeek* magazine. Before coming to *BusinessWeek,* Lehman held editorial positions at *Architects Newspaper* and *Radar* magazine. She is a graduate of Duke University where she covered sports for the daily paper, the *Chronicle.*

DEXTER ROBERTS is the Asia News editor and China bureau chief for *BusinessWeek.* He started reporting for *BusinessWeek* in China in 1995 and became Beijing bureau chief in 1998. In more than a decade of reporting from China, he has covered everything from politics and trade, to labor, energy, and autos. Mr. Roberts has won numerous journalism awards, including Overseas Press Club awards and citations, the Sidney Hillman Foundation prize, Human Rights Press awards, and Society of Publishers in Asia editorial excellence awards.

Mr. Roberts has a Bachelor of Arts in political science from Stanford University where he was a National Merit Scholar, and a Master of International Affairs focusing on China and journalism from Columbia University. He has studied Chinese at Stanford and at National Taiwan Normal University's Mandarin Training Center. He is from Missoula, Montana.

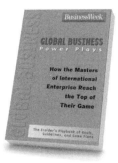